YOUTH NIGHTS MADE EASIER

Edited by
Leo Symmank and Karen Jurgensen

Publishing House
St. Louis

Acknowledgments

It is with warm affection that I acknowledge the special contribution that was made to the compilation of this book by Marcia Earhart, Karen Jurgensen, and Kathy Pratt. All three were key in preparing the manuscript for publication.

I extend my thanks also to all the writers who contributed planned youth nights to this book. Theirs is a truly significant gift to all of us who work with young people in the ministry of the church.

Leo Symmank

Unless otherwise indicated, the Scripture quotations in this publication are from the Good News Bible, the Bible in TODAY'S ENGLISH VERSION. Copyright © American Bible Society 1966, 1971, 1976. Used by permission.

Biblical references marked RSV are from the Revised Standard Version of the Bible, copyrighted 1946, 1952 © 1971, 1973. Used by permission.

Permission to reproduce materials in this book should be requested from the Board for Youth Services, The Lutheran Church—Missouri Synod, 1333 S. Kirkwood Road, St. Louis, MO 63122 — (314)965-9000.

Copyright © 1986 Concordia Publishing House
3558 S. Jefferson Avenue, St. Louis, MO 63118
Manufactured in the United States of America

All rights reserved. No part of this publication may be reproduced, stored in a retrieval system, or transmitted, in any form or by any means, electronic, mechanical, photocopying, recording, or otherwise, without the prior written permission of Concordia Publishing House.

1 2 3 4 5 6 7 8 9 10   MAL   95 94 93 92 91 90 89 88 87 86

Contents

Foreword   5

Introduction

    Planning the Year's Program with the Help of This Book   7

    What Constitutes a Good Youth Night?   7

    The Small Youth Group   7

    Getting at Youth Needs   8

    Conclusion   8

Youth Nights

    Loneliness: Is Anybody Listening? Does Anybody Care?   11

    Family Trouble: The Youth Group as a Friend   12

    Outrage: Lord, What Can We Do to Help?   13

    Closed Minds: Checking Out Prejudices   14

    Joy: That's Good News   16

    An Advent Ad   17

    Mountains and Valleys (Highs and Lows in Life)   20

    Behind the Wheel   24

    Decisions Involving Jobs   28

    Let's Be Friends (Nondating Relationships)   31

    My Body—My Buddy (My Sexuality)   35

    Stumbling Around in the Dark (Light and Darkness in Life)   39

    Talking in the Light (An Advent Night)   41

    In Whose Image? (An Epiphany Night)   43

    Growing Through Grieving   45

    Life Is Forgiving   48

    The Feelings of Others (Communicating Feelings)   51

    Give It All You've Got (Money and Our Giving)   54

    A Time for Giving (An Advent Night)   56

    Christmas Prayer   59

Day by Day: O Dear Lord, Three Things I Pray (An Epiphany Night)	61
It's Not Easy Being Green (Each Person a Special Child of God)	66
Family "Is Shoes" (Strengths and Weaknesses Within One's Family)	69
Barefootin' and Carefootin' (Appreciating our Family)	71
The Shoelace Acceptance—Do It Now! (Worth of Individual Family Members)	74
Shoes . . . I Know Where You're Coming From (Empathy in Relationships)	77
Careful Saints! (People Who Care)	80
Footsteps and Footprints (Following in Jesus' Steps)	82
Stress and School	85
Good Grief?	87
Called to Comfort	90
Success with a Capital "S"	93
My Success Goal	96
Lusty Lady, Cradled Lamb (Jesus' Love as Strength for Our Loving)	97
Guilty (God's Forgiveness)	100
Remember the Able/Disabled	103
Ear Wax and Cotton (Being Better Listeners)	106
Money Is Power?	110
I Am My Job	113
Bare Branches—A Chance to Cry (Sharing Struggles and Hurts)	116
Index	119

Foreword

Can your ministry really be made "easier"? For those involved in ministry to young people, we know that it can be a strenuous, time-consuming responsibility. And no specific book or stack of resource materials will suddenly change that fact.

Resources like this book, however, do help the leaders of youth ministry groups in parishes by providing useful, Christ-centered materials which make sessions more meaningful because they are directed to the needs of young people today.

Some may remark that what youth ministry needs these days is *not* another book on "how to" do youth ministry! There continues to be a stream of new resources in this area, some good, and some not so good. But the activities in this resource book are different in the sense that all of them have been tried out by real youth groups. They effectively involve young people in ministry where they are.

These youth nights come from previous issues of *Resources for Youth Ministry*, published by the Board for Youth Services, The Lutheran Church—Missouri Synod, 1333 S. Kirkwood Road, St. Louis, MO, 63122. They are edited by Pastor Leo Symmank, who has applied the sensitivity and insight of over 30 years experience in youth ministry to select and edit these programmatic resources, creating activities with specific, stated objectives. His experience is reflected in the end product.

Enjoy these pages. Adapt them! Make them fit your own needs. They will help you recognize that youth ministry can be "easier" as you allow the Spirit to work on others through you.

Richard W. Bimler
Executive Secretary
Board for Youth Services
The Lutheran Church—Missouri Synod
St. Louis, MO

Introduction

Planning the Year's Program with the Help of This Book

"What are we going to do at our youth meetings next quarter?" is a frequently asked question by those in youth ministry. This book provides you with a variety of choices to meet your planning needs. It can contribute a major part to your year's program. Most of the work has been done for you. Look at the needs of your youth and choose youth nights that best meet those needs. If you want help in discovering the needs of the youth in your parish, this book offers some helpful suggestions.

In addition, you will want to plan some special events. This may be a retreat or summer trip, several service projects, a summer work camp, a special series of Bible studies, a special worship service involving the congregation, or some event that has become a tradition in your church.

Even if the congregation chooses not to have a formally structured youth organization, most congregations will want to bring youth together in groups occasionally for Bible study, service projects, and fellowship. The organized group, however, continues to be the most common form for achieving youth interaction in an effective, ongoing manner.

The organized group primarily gives youth the opportunity

- to develop leadership skills;
- to plan their own worship and Bible study;
- to meet regularly with other youth from their congregation for Christian fellowship;
- to develop identity and a sense of belonging;
- to be part of the decision-making process as they plan events for their organization;
- to express their views and values; and
- to influence the mission and ministry of the congregation, especially if the organized youth group is in some way structurally linked with the congregation's decision-making groups.

What Constitutes a Good Youth Night?

The answer will not be the same for every group, because needs and interests vary. Some things can be considered to enhance a youth night.

Did you ever hear this conversation: "What are we going to do to get the kids to come?" "Yea, they come to the socials, but few show up for topic studies and business meetings."

It is surprising that many youth groups still have a schedule that looks something like this:

First Sunday—Business Meeting
Second Sunday—Topic Discussion
Third Sunday—Bible Study
Fourth Sunday—Social

More and more youth groups are discontinuing the practice of devoting a whole afternoon or evening to business. Sometimes a retreat or an afternoon and evening at the church is used to surface needs and expectations of the group. The officers or a program committee then plan the programs for the next three to six months and involve different people in planning the details and implementing the events.

The planned youth nights in this book generally include the following ingredients:

1. Some icebreaker activity—frequently this introduces the theme for the evening.
2. A short Bible study or a topic discussion related to what the Scriptures say on a particular subject.
3. A brief devotion.
4. Some recreational activity.
5. Fellowship and refreshments.

The order of these activities is not always the same. In fact, it is helpful to vary the order.

The Small Youth Group

Some people may think that their church does not have enough youth for a youth group. Even if a congregation has only three or four high school youth, these youth may want to meet together for fellowship and for sharing their doubts and faith. I know of congregations with as few as three to five youth who meet together regularly and feel good about it. Sometimes a smaller group can invite and host the youth of a neighboring church for an event.

The planned youth nights in this book have been designed to accommodate youth groups that have over six or eight in their group. But when a given activity can best be carried out in a smaller group, the writer will suggest dividing into groups of five or six. These small group activities are, in a real sense, an affirmation to the small youth group. When youth are asked to share some aspect of their Christian faith, the small group has the advantage of hearing from everyone in its group.

Jesus says, "Where two or three are gathered together in my name, there am I in the midst of them." These words should give special comfort and joy to the small group.

Getting at Youth Needs

Youth leaders in the congregation can improve their ministry with young people by surveying the specific needs of the youth associated with their congregation's ministry. Various survey instruments are available. One of these is "The Needs Assessment Kit," available from Youth Ministry Materials, 1333 South Kirkwood Road, St. Louis, MO 63122 (cost $5). The survey can be administered to a group of youth in approximately one hour. It surveys primary needs in five areas: Social, Spiritual, Personal, Growth, and Ministry.

Here is another survey technique you may want to use with your youth:

1. Have youth sit in a semicircle or in classroom style.
2. Give all the participants a pencil and a 4" x 6" card.
3. Ask the youth to think of someone in their youth group whom they know well.
4. Have them write on a 4" x 6" card two or three needs of this person. Allow time for participants to reflect and to write. (*Note:* Instruct participants to name only those needs with which the friend would agree. Sometimes we tend to impose needs on others: "She needs to stop drinking so much." "He needs to be in Bible class." Perhaps this is true, but until the friend is willing to acknowledge it as a need, it will be most difficult to serve that need.)
5. Next ask participants to think of a second youth and again list two or three of his or her most important needs.
6. Finally, ask the participants to list three or four of their own most important needs on the card.
7. Prepare to write these needs on a chalkboard or on sheets of newsprint in front of the group.
8. Ask each person to name one of the needs from his or her card. It does not have to be the one at the top of the list. Begin with the person on your left and continue to ask each person in turn to name only one need from his or her list. Tell the participants that if another person has already named one of their needs to cross this need off their lists and choose one that has not yet been posted on the chalkboard. Continue the process until all the needs are listed. The total list may be 30 or more. Number the needs on the chalkboard or newsprint.
9. Ask participants again to think of their two friends and their needs, also their personal needs, plus the needs of others in their youth group.
10. Now ask participants to select from the entire list of needs, the eight needs that they believe are the most common and most important needs of their youth group. (Give group members time to reflect and to write the numbers of their needs on their 4" x 6" cards.)
11. Call out each need and number. Then record behind it the number of votes cast for each.
12. Survey the results and see which are the six or seven primary needs (those with the highest votes) of your youth group according to this survey.

You may want to talk about what activities could be planned to help meet these six or seven most common needs.

Use the needs list to assist you to develop a program for your group for the next six months or year.

Conclusion

Once you have selected the planned youth night that coincides with your group's needs, you will want to evaluate how each part of the planned event supports your purposes. You may want to eliminate, adapt, or rework. Whatever you decide, involve youth in the process. What did they find especially helpful? What would they change? You may want to date and save these notes. If you have a lot to say, insert a page with notes. In the future you, or someone who may follow you, could make good use of the experience you have gained.

The activities in this book are as varied as the number of contributors. Yet the underlying goal of each is to create a setting and provide activities through which the relationship between the participants and the Lord is strengthened, and friendships among young people are deepened.

While interesting activities can help, the adult leader's faith in the Lord plays a key role in making these activities reflect Christ's love. To the glory of God, may you express that faith throughout your work with young people.

Loneliness: Is Anybody Listening? Does Anybody Care?

by Rich Bimler and Steve Sonnenberg

Objectives

To surface the feelings of loneliness and despair
To experience some ways of dealing with loneliness
To rejoice in the presence of Christ in our lives!

Materials Needed

Lists of magazine titles
Bibles

Let's Get Started

1. Begin the session with a prayer. Then read Rom. 5:1–11 and reflect on the fact that God has made each of us His friend through Christ. (10 min.)
2. Get into groups of four or five people and pass out the following list of magazines. Feel free to add to or subtract from this list.

    ___Rolling Stone   ___Glamour   ___TV Guide
    ___Popular Mechanics   ___Sixteen   ___Time
    ___Reader's Digest   ___Hot Rod   ___Mad
    ___Better Homes and Gardens ___Parents   ___Surfer
    ___Sports Illustrated   ___Holiday   ___Youth

3. Have each person respond to the following questions. Share these responses in the small groups.
    a. What magazine(s) best describe(s) you right now? Why? Which one(s) best describe(s) the way you would like to be?
    b. Which magazine(s) is the farthest from your likes, personality, and feelings?
    c. If you had available one free page of advertising in one of these magazines, which magazine would you choose, and what would your ad say? (15 min.)
4. The Scriptures share feelings of loneliness in many ways. We remember Christ's loneliness on the cross. We reflect on Peter's feelings after his denial. We can still see Judas and his struggles after the betrayal. Take a look at the examples found in Matt. 26:30–56; 69–75; 27:1–50. Some questions to reflect on:
    a. What caused this loneliness or despair?
    b. What resulted from these feelings and why?
    c. How do you work through your feelings of loneliness?

    It is interesting to note that both Peter and Judas struggled with feelings of guilt and despair. Judas turned these feelings into himself; Peter saw the forgiveness of Christ and found new comfort and power because he turned his feelings over to the Lord. (30 min.)
5. In pairs, have each person share with a partner some additional feelings of loneliness and despair. Encourage the teams to share such thoughts as:
    When do you feel most lonely?
    What can you do to help others struggle through their feelings of loneliness?
    Are feelings "bad"? Are they "abnormal"?
    Think of people you know who are lonely. How can you respond to them in love and concern? (20 min.)

Other Options

1. Have a study on Baptism. How does this Sacrament relate to loneliness?
2. Develop a Confession-Absolution service together. Write it up and share it on a Sunday

morning.
3. As a group, go and visit the "lonely" in your neighborhood. What people need you right now? Plan to visit shut-ins or older folk each month.
4. Set apart some time each day for reflection on the Scripture and for sharing your faith with one other person.
5. Listen to some popular songs together. Pick out the cries of despair and loneliness. Discuss what you would say to the people the music portrays.

TO KNOW GOD IS TO KNOW THAT EVEN WHEN YOU ARE ALONE—YOU'RE NOT!

Family Trouble: The Youth Group as a Friend

by Rich Bimler and Steve Sonnenberg

Objectives
To provide an opportunity for sharing of self
To practice the skill of listening
To experience a feeling of community

Materials Needed
Bibles
Pencils
"All About Me" and "Discovery" sheets for each person
Magic markers or crayons
Strips of paper (14" x 2")
Stapler

(If the two handouts cannot be duplicated, write the questions on a chalkboard or on newsprint; have plain paper available for the answers.)

Let's Get Started

1. Distribute the following prepared-in-advance "All About Me" sheets. (Make sure you've left plenty of room for answers.) Have everyone fill in their responses. (10 min.)

All About Me

a. Some of the unique (different) things about me are . . .
b. Some of the special things I can contribute are . . .
c. I feel bad about myself when . . .
d. One of the most beautiful things I've ever seen is . . .
e. One of the ugliest things I've ever seen is . . .
f. One of the most significant persons in my life is . . .
g. If I could change my family, I would . . .
h. If I could change the church, I would . . .

2. Have participants form groups of three people. One person at a time should share the things he or she has written. The other two people in the group will serve as listeners, focusing their attention on the person who is speaking. The listeners should try to help the speaker understand his or her feelings. They should not give out answers or "judge" how the person feels. Acceptance is the key. After five minutes the speaker will become a listener, and one of the listeners will have a chance to speak. Make sure everyone in the group has a chance to speak. (15 min.)

3. Bring the group back together in a circle. Pass out the "Discovery" sheets (these should be prepared in advance) and have everyone complete the sentences on them. (10 min.)

Discovery Sheet

    a. I learned that . . .
    b. I was surprised that I . . .
    c. I felt sad when . . .
    d. I enjoyed . . .
    e. I never knew . . .
    f. I plan to . . .

4. Moving around the circle, have the people who feel comfortable doing so share some of their discoveries. Try to find ways to affirm members of the group. (10 min.)
5. Move to a comfortable worship setting. Hand out the strips of paper and pens. On each slip have participants write the name of a person who is important to them, one per slip. (Have plenty of extra slips on hand.) Using the stapler, make a long paper chain. This could be draped on the altar or held by the group (put your wrists through the links and sit in a circle). (5 min.)
6. Read Rom. 12:9–12. Discuss what it means to be "bound" to those who are important to you. Have youth think of some special thing that could be done for one of the people named on the chain link. Have them plan to do this during the coming week. (15 min.)
7. Close with a blessing and a "oneness experience"—have participants walk back to the meeting area with eyes closed, one hand on the chain, the other holding on to another person's hand. The leader should see that everyone gets back "safely." (5 min.)

Other Options

1. Have a group night where everyone brings a "significant adult" along. Provide some opportunities for real sharing.
2. Encourage youth to surprise a family member with an act of love.

Outrage: Lord, What Can We Do to Help?

by Rich Bimler and Steve Sonnenberg

Objectives

To discuss ways of meeting some of the needs of people
To become more sensitive to people
To take some action concerning world hunger

Materials Needed

    Bibles
    Hunger materials

Background

This is a program aimed at involving the youth group specifically in world hunger concerns. Many good materials are available from the Board for Social Ministry of The Lutheran Church—Missouri Synod (LCMS), 1333 South Kirkwood Road, St. Louis, MO 63122. These materials should be ordered ahead of the meeting and distributed at the meeting. Ask each person to bring two food items to the meeting—one food item they like and one they do not like.

Let's Get Started

1. Begin with a prayer: *Lord, some people have appetites, but no food; others have food, but no appetites. Thanks Lord for giving us both food and appetites. Help us to share both physical food and spiritual food with people throughout the world. Amen.*
2. Biblical passages for discussion: Deut. 15:7–11; Amos 4; Micah 6:8–16; Matt. 25:31–46; Acts 2:42–47. In small groups discuss how these passages are relevant to world hunger. (15 min.)
3. Discuss the food items that were brought. Why do we like some foods but not others? Do we have a tendency to give away "items" we don't like or need rather than giving what other people really need? Decide what to do with the food items you've collected. (15 min.)
4. Invite a guest to come in to discuss world hunger with you—a school teacher, missionary, pastor, government official, farmer, or the like. Or better yet, have a panel of people who are willing to discuss their insights and feelings about world hunger. (30 min.)
5. Discuss ways that your group could make your parish more aware of world hunger, for example, by conducting Bible studies, hosting a "nonbanquet," where no food is served and the savings go to a world hunger project, holding a hunger workshop or hike, going on a hunger retreat, sending out a hunger information newsletter, or holding special worship services. (15 min.)
6. As a group or in teams, decide on one specific hunger project to follow through on for the next six months, for example, hikes, fasts, collection of money, a school project, or a consciousness-raising program. The point is to make a specific commitment to world hunger through a reachable, realistic goal. (10 min.)
7. A closing prayer. Collect the thoughts the group has about the study and discussion and have a leader include them in a prayer. Specific prayers may also be requested.

Other Options

1. Films on world hunger are available through the LCMS's Social Ministry office.
2. Have a hunger banquet for your parish. Serve only rice or bread and water. Or have an Un-dinner. Using the following menu, invite the congregation to supper and discuss world hunger. Have everyone order 13 cents worth of food, the daily food budget for many people in the world.

    Water—1 cent a glass
    Coffee—6 cents
       (sugar 2 cents, milk 2 cents)
    Saltines—1 cent a serving
    American cheese—6 cents a serving
    Radishes—1 cent a serving
    Olives—2 cents a serving

    Tangerines—8 cents a serving

    Hard-boiled egg—6 cent each
    Carrots—3 cents a serving
    Sweet pickles—2 cents a serving
    Raisins—9 cents a serving
    Cookies—3 cents a serving

    (Menu taken from *PROBE Newsletter*, February 1975)
3. Have each family in your parish skip one meal or cut out snacks. Collect the money they saved on groceries by doing this and contribute it to a world hunger project.

Closed Minds: Checking Out Prejudices

by Rich Bimler and Steve Sonnenberg

Objectives

To help young people explore their prejudices
To write some "beatitudes"

Materials Needed

Bibles
Paper and pencils
3" x 5" cards (one for each person)
Pins

Let's Get Started

1. For this Bible study we suggest that the NIV, RSV, TEV, or *The Living Bible* be used because of their contemporary wording. Read Matt. 5:1-12. Why did Jesus mention these specific qualities? What would the blessings sound like today? What is the real meaning of these blessings? Have the group write their own beatitudes. For example, "Blessed are (nurses) for they (care)." (15 min.)

2. Divide the participants into groups of six. Tell them to listen to and follow these directions carefully:

    "Your group is responsible for the future of humankind. The Pentagon has notified you that in about 30 minutes your neighborhood will be completely destroyed. It has been agreed that no one from among your committee will be saved, but it is up to your group to determine who will be. There are 10 candidates for the six places in the Fallout Shelter. You must decide, on the basis of the following information, who will be saved. If you have not arrived at a decision in 30 minutes, everyone will die. The 10 candidates are (*you may want to duplicate this information; otherwise, put it on newsprint or on a chalkboard so that everyone can see it*):

    a. A pregnant high school drop-out with a low I.Q.
    b. A 47-year-old nuclear scientist, largely responsible for the development of the nuclear weapons in use
    c. A television celebrity who hosts talk shows
    d. A 50-year-old alcoholic priest
    e. A 20-year-old militant black architect
    f. A very successful woman doctor incapable of having children
    g. A law student and his wife, who has leukemia and less than a year to live (They refuse to be separated.)
    h. A famous 60-year-old psychologist and author
    i. A 28-year-old policeman who is a former Olympic athlete and who is presently awaiting a hearing on the charge of brutality"

    Allow 30 minutes for participants to present their lists to you.

3. Give each group an opportunity to share their list and the reasons for their choices. Do they feel they have the "right" answer? What assumptions did they make about these 10 people? Did they assume that only the militant architect was black? Were the scientist, TV personality, and architect women or men? (10 min.)

4. Have each group of six make a list of the various prejudices that surfaced in their discussion. You may wish to suggest that each person evaluate his or her own prejudices by using the "Discovery" statements in the unit on "Family Trouble: The Youth Group as a Friend." Or complete the following "I wonder" statements: "I wonder if . . . ," "I wonder how . . . ," "I wonder when . . . ," "I wonder whether . . ." Whichever method is used, help everyone take a long hard look at the prejudices they expressed. No attempt should be made to "put people down" because they are honest enough to admit their prejudices. The goal is that once prejudices have been exposed individuals can begin to work on overcoming them. (10 min.)

5. As a closing read James 2:1-13. Discuss the evidence of true faith. Try substituting names for rich and poor and the descriptive characteristics of each in order to see what is being said concerning different kinds of people. Close with a prayer for "unlikely saints" (people mentioned in the group's beatitudes or people we see everyday and may not appreciate, for example, teachers, funny people who help us laugh, people who are gracious in their old age, martyrs without labels). End by having everyone make a name tag from a 3" x 5" card. On this card have youth put their names and an "ing" adjective describing what they are trying to become in light of the things discussed in this program. Have them put the

tags on and wear them for awhile. (15 min.)

Other Options

1. Have a "senior citizens" or "tot" party—or invite both groups together.
2. Tape record the worship service and share it with a shut-in.
3. Sponsor an advertisement in the newspaper supporting some issue that is not getting a fair hearing.
4. Have a county nurse come to a meeting to share about the special needs of some of the people in your community.

Joy: That's Good News

by Rich Bimler and Steve Sonnenberg

Objectives

To share the joy we have in Christ Jesus
To explore ways of sharing with others this joy we have
To have fun together as God's people

Materials Needed

    Bibles
    Magazines
    Newspapers
    Pencils
    Paper
    Glue

Background

This program attempts to structure a setting where people will be able to share their faith with each other in a Spirit-filled atmosphere. Before your meeting, ask everyone to come with some "good news/bad news" jokes.

Let's Get Started

1. As people arrive, have them search through lots of magazines and newspapers for words and pictures that say "Good News" to them. On posterboard or newsprint, make one huge collage out of these words and pictures. Display it during your meeting, and leave it up for other groups to see. (15 min.)
2. Discuss "Good News." What is it? Martin Marty says that to many people today the Gospel may be good, but it's not news. Have youth share their feelings about this. (10 min.)
3. Have youth share some of the "good news/bad news" jokes they know. Discuss them in light of the Good News of the Scriptures. (For example, Johnny Carson says, "I've got good news and bad news for you. First, the bad: there ain't no good news!" Ask youth, "What does this say to your faith?") (20 min.)
4. Is our world more concerned with good news or with bad news? Ask youth what they see or hear more of. Why? Have them check on the amount of good news and bad news in today's paper. Have newspapers available for the group to cut out good and bad news. (15 min.)
5. The joy for Christians to share is that we really do have Good News—in Christ Jesus.

Have each person take his or her Bible and look through it. Record as many Good News passages as possible. Then let the group also look for some bad news in Scripture—in terms of our sinful nature, etc. Share these passages in one large group or in smaller groups of three or four people. (25 min.)
6. Another joy for the people of God is that He allows us to be messengers of the Good News to people around us. Have youth share with one other person some Good News that has happened in their lives recently—in their families, school, or church. (10 min.)
7. Now, with that same person, have them share the name of someone to whom they really feel they are or can be bearers of the Good News, or the name of someone with whom they need to share the Good News. (10 min.)
8. "No news is no Good News!" For some Christians it is difficult to verbalize their faith with others. Discuss why this is true. Discuss ways that the youth might help others share their faith verbally. (10 min.)
9. Roleplay some situations to surface your feelings concerning witnessing. Some possible situations follow. (25 min.)
    a. A good friend of yours asks you why you go to church. She thinks it's ridiculous.
    b. Two people are talking. One says that religion is a private matter and that it's not necessary to talk to others about faith.
    c. Your youth group is asked to make calls with the Evangelism Committee. Two kids show up. Later, your dad complains to you that it is terrible that only two kids came. He accuses the youth of being lazy and self-centered.
    d. A person stops you on the street and asks, "Are you saved?" and begins to warn you that you had better repent.
10. Sharing our faith in joy is not something that we must do. It is something we are privileged and allowed to do through the Spirit. Before you break for the evening, have each youth write the name of a person he or she knows personally. What would he or she like to say to this person about Jesus Christ? Have each person write a contract with him/herself, committing him/herself to talk with that person during the coming week. (10 min.)
11. To close, form a large circle and ask for voluntary prayers from the group. Close with the Lord's Prayer and the Benediction. Do it with joy! (5 min.)

Other Options

1. Invite your Evangelism Committee to come and talk with your group about evangelism plans in your parish.
2. Take a survey of your church or neighborhood. Find out why people do or do not attend church.
3. Discuss with your pastor ways of making your worship services as joyful as possible. You might have some suggestions to share with him.
4. Make a banner or poster for your church. Title it, "And here's the Good News!" Encourage members to write their favorite Good News words from Scripture and daily life on the banner. Keep it up as a visible sign of the Good News.

An Advent Ad

by Karen Melang

Objectives

To look at John, the walking billboard for Christ, and at our church community, past and present, as an ad also

To see the community of the church as caring out loud about each other

Materials Needed

Bibles

Introduction to Topic

Advertising is a great part of the American way of life, and never more so than right before Christmas. One of the important Advent figures of the church's history is John the Baptist, who, in an odd and intriguing and surprisingly effective way, was a walking ADvent AD for our Lord. This youth night focuses on John, the walking billboard for Christ, and on our church community, past and present, as an ad also.

Icebreaker/Get-Acquainted Activity

Youth should form two circles, one inside the other, with people facing each other in pairs. Have them spend about two minutes talking with each other about what each thinks is the most disgusting, despicable, lousy, tasteless, or whatever, TV commercial and why. Let the leader call time at two minutes, and have the outside circle rotate clockwise to the next person and share again.

The youth may find themselves with more than one "rotten" favorite. Or they might find a grand winner in the group. At any rate, they'll find out something about the others in their community.

Learning Experience

Have youth divide into groups of five or six. Tell them to read the following and choose the one they think is most true. Then have them discuss John's liabilities and assets as an ad for Jesus.

1. Read John 1:6–8, 19–28. If John were advertising Jesus today, I think
   ___with so many people interested in religion, lots of people would listen and believe.
   ___with so many people wary of people who dress and act differently, people would write John off as a "weirdo."
   ___with so many people aware of rip-off religious cults, John wouldn't get much of a following.

2. John was well aware of his status as a billboard or advertisement (John 1:27; 3:25–30). But he is not the only ad around. Briefly describe the last time it occurred to you that you should or should not do a certain thing because you were a Christian. Did you feel
   ___supported by others?
   ___guilty?
   ___ashamed?
   ___affirmed in your faith?

3. Being a billboard can be a lonely business. See Matt. 11:2–3. John was at a low ebb. He had been imprisoned for speaking against Herod's immoral relationship with his sister-in-law. John began to wonder if his life as an ad had been worthwhile, and even if there had been truth in his advertising. But Jesus' words built John up again: "I assure you that John the Baptist is greater than any man who has ever lived" (Matt. 11:11).

The community of the church is for caring out loud about each other. Encourage each participant to mention to the others in his or her small group something that each of them has done for him or her, an insight the person has shared, or some way the person has been helpful either tonight or at some other time.

Optional Activity

Develop a TV commercial for your church. Forget about service times and instead tell about the gifts (forgiveness, peace, community, caring) that are being given away at your church. Keeping John's message in mind (Luke 3:7–14), think, too, about the risks and costs of being the church.

Recreation

The following games are all taken from *The New Games Book*, edited by Andrew Fluegelman and published by Doubleday. It is certainly a book worth having and using. It's all about the community at play, and what community has more reason to play and celebrate being alive together than the holy Christian church—all of us? Get your hands on the book, and in the meantime . . .

Stand Up

Start by sitting on the ground, knees bent, and back to back with one partner. Link elbows and stand up. Sounds easy enough, right? Give it a try. Now try it in groups of three.

New Games says that four stander-uppers is a genuine accomplishment; and five, a rare event. The more people, the more giggling, cooperation, struggling, and fun there'll be. How about trying for a record number in a mass stand up?

Fox and Squirrel

Three balls are needed for this game. Two balls, the "foxes," should be similar, and the third, the "squirrel," should be different and probably smaller.

Standing in a circle, begin to pass the "foxes" from player to player one at a time. "Foxes" may be passed in opposite directions or one behind the other but must always be passed only from one player to the next. Practice passing the "foxes," working up to top speed and throwing in a reversal now and again to keep everyone alert.

Now enter the "squirrel." The "squirrel" can leap as well as run and so can be thrown across the circle to any player as well as being passed from person to person. The object of the game is to catch the "squirrel" by tagging whoever is holding it with one or both of the "foxes."

To keep things straight, each player should shout "fox" or "squirrel" as he or she passes one of the balls.

New Games says not to expect much peace and quiet in this "forest" since the game seems to be played "at near panic levels."

Prui (Pronounced PROO-ee)

Have all youth present close their eyes and mill about. When a person bumps into another, he or she shakes the other's hand and asks, "Prui?" and the other person responds by repeating the question. When everyone is milling nicely about, the referee whispers to one player that he or she is the Prui. The Prui can see, but he or she has exchanged sight for speech and can't talk. Now when someone bumps into the Prui, shakes his or her hand, and asks, "Prui?" there is no response. The person who has bumped into the Prui then joins hands with him or her and becomes a part of the Prui. Both now stand with hands joined, eyes open, but mute.

So the Prui grows. Whenever a person with eyes closed runs into clasped hands, he or she knows that he or she has found the Prui. With eyes closed, that person feels his or her way to one end of the line and joins it, then stands with hands joined with the others, eyes open, mouth closed.

When all have found each other, all give a rousing cheer and move with hands still joined on an Advent journey to the worship area.

Worship

Let the whole group gather around the appropriately lit Advent wreath.

> **Leader:** Today is a celebration of our caring community. We celebrate and are thankful, particularly for the life of John the Baptist, the ADvent AD. We thank God for John's willingness to be different, to speak the truth no matter what, for his courage in sharing even his doubts, for his willingness to be only a billboard and not the main event.
> **Sing:** "On Jordan's Bank the Baptist's Cry"
> **Leader:** We celebrate also those saints—living or dead—who light up our lives. Let each one share with one other person what one saint has meant in his or her life. The saint can be a grandparent, friend, teacher, or person here today—anyone who has been an ad for Christ in word and deed, someone who has brought us to or helped us live in the community of the church.

A simple prayer of thanksgiving may be prayed for all those who have pointed us to Jesus and who were not ashamed to be walking commercials for His care.

If time permits, and if you did the optional learning activity, one or more of the commercials for your church might be presented. Or how about making plans to present them at an Advent service—or on TV?

Afterglow

Ethnic Advent cookies—Mexican wedding cakes, krumkake, or springerle—might be a fun way to celebrate the diversity—even in tastes—of our miraculously large family, the church.

(*Note:* At this time of the year even one more cookie might be more than the baker in the house can handle. If the youths in charge of supplying the snacks for this event are not the bakers, have them keep this in mind. Remember that the youth group can talk over a couple of huge bowls of popcorn just as happily.)

Add a batch of hot cocoa and voilà . . .

Mountains and Valleys
(Highs and Lows in Life)

by Bill Ameiss

Objectives

To think through the Transfiguration event
To get in touch with some of our own lows and highs
To recognize the presence of the Savior in both highs and lows

Materials Needed

5" x 7" index cards
Fine-point markers
Newsprint
Duplicated Bible text
Duplicated Bible study

Introduction to Topic

The last Sunday after the Epiphany is the Sunday of the Transfiguration. Transfiguration hardly qualifies as one of the most widely known events in the church year. If you were giving a Transfiguration party, how many people would really know what you were celebrating? Yet, the event is remembered in one way by a good number of people. Transfiguration gives to us the term "mountaintop experience," a reference to the momentous events by which our Lord's glory was seen in a vision with Moses and Elijah. The term "mountaintop experience" may be better known than the Transfiguration event that created it. The term is a good handle. Who has never experienced a real "high," a "mountaintop experience"—a really great experience that makes us feel "on top of the world"?

And who has never been through a really bad situation, a low point, a real valley? Mountains and valleys, high points and low points, are a part of our lives.

The following activities offer us a chance to think through the Transfiguration event, to get in touch with some of our own lows and highs, and to recognize the presence of the Savior in the middle of it all. The activities are planned within a two-hour framework and are designed for groups in which the members at least know each other by name.

Icebreaker/Get-Acquainted Activity: the Untag (30 min.)

The goal of this activity is to help those present begin to think about some of the "high points" and "low points," mountains and valleys, in their own lives. Pass out a 5" x 7" note card (blank cards are best) and fine-point felt-tip markers to each person. Post horizontally, in full view, a sheet of newsprint (24" x 36") as a replica of the card. As you introduce each of the four parts of the Untag, write the key word on the large piece of newsprint so that the Untag design is seen by the group.

Making the Untag

Give the following directions: "You have all heard of name tags before. You've probably all made them. This isn't a name tag (*referring to the large newsprint replica*), this is an untag, a name tag without a name on it, not even 'un!'

"In the upper right-hand corner of your untag I want you to draw a symbol that depicts a real high point, a mountaintop experience in your life. It could be a vacation experience, or something from school or home. It could be something you remember from worship or a retreat. Draw a symbol that captures that high point for you."

(*Write the words "HIGH POINT" in the upper right-hand corner of the newsprint replica of the untag. Allow a minute or two for each person to complete the symbol. Then continue:*)

"Think of the high point once again. Try to remember especially the feelings that went with it. What feeling is most real in your memory: excitement, awe, or surprise? Whatever that feeling, write it down, in the lower right-hand corner of the untag. Just a word or two will do."

(*Write "FEELING" in the lower right-hand corner. Allow a minute or so for completion. Then continue:*) "Now try to think of a time in your life that was really a low point for you, a real valley. Perhaps that valley took place at school, or maybe it happened at home. It could have occurred at church, with the youth group, or even with the kids in the neighborhood. In the upper left-hand corner of the untag, draw a symbol that represents that low point, that valley in your life."

(*Write the words "LOW POINT" in the upper left-hand corner of the newsprint replica of the untag. After a minute or two, continue:*)

"I'm sure you're still thinking about the low point. It can be a less than pleasant memory. But it can also be helpful. As you think about the low point, try to get in touch with the feelings you remember from that event. Maybe you experienced feelings of frustration, or failure; perhaps, defeat or rejection. Whatever the feeling or feelings that remain in your memories, write them down in the lower left-hand corner of the untag."

(*Add the word "FEELINGS" to the lower left-hand corner of the newsprint replica of the untag and wait a moment for all to finish before moving on to the directions for sharing the untag.*)

Sharing the Untag

After each person has finished the untag, divide the youth (by random count-off) into groups of four to six for sharing. These groups will stay together for the untag sharing and the learning experience. Give each group a minute or two to get settled in its own "place." Chairs are optional; the group members need to be close enough to share easily.

Directions could be given as follows: "Each person in your share group will have three or four minutes to share as much of his or her untag as he or she feels comfortable doing. Give your full attention to the person sharing. This is not the time for rebuttal or discussion. It is the time for careful and sensitive listening. As you share your untag, explain the symbolism in the high point and the low point, and whatever other information you need to communicate the events. As you share the feelings connected with the experiences, you might add a sentence or two to say something about what the experiences meant to you."

"Here is what I mean . . . ." (*Share your untag at this point. After sharing your untag, remind group members that they will have 12 to 15 minutes for their sharing time.*)

Bible Study on Matt. 17:1-8 (30 min.)

Six days later Jesus took with Him Peter and the brothers James and John and led them up a high mountain where they were alone. As they looked on, a change came over Jesus:

His face was shining like the sun, and His clothes were dazzling white. Then the three

disciples saw Moses and Elijah talking with Jesus. So Peter spoke up and said to Jesus, "Lord, how good it is that we are here! If You wish, I will make three tents here, one for You, one for Moses, and one for Elijah."

While He was talking, a shining cloud came over them and a voice said from the clouds: "This is my own dear Son, with whom I am well pleased—listen to Him!"

When the disciples heard the voice, they were so terrified that they threw themselves face down to the ground. Jesus came to them and touched them. "Get up," He said. "Don't be afraid!" So they looked up and saw no one there but Jesus.

(The text above and the following Bible study should be duplicated for each person. When the untag sharing has been completed, hand out copies of the Bible study.)

Thinking About the Transfiguration

A. To me, it seems that the "high point" in this experience for Peter, James, and John must have been
   ___the fact that they, rather than the other disciples, were on the mountaintop;
   ___the appearance of the two Old Testament leaders there with Jesus;
   ___the spectacular nature of the whole event—its bright lights, "clothes as white as light," "shining cloud," and "voice"; or
   ___the voice from the cloud, saying, "This is My own dear Son, with whom I am well pleased; listen to Him!"

B. If I would ask God just one question about this whole event, it would be
   ___Why all the drama, the light, the voice, the cloud?
   ___Why did You pick Moses and Elijah; why not someone like Adam or Abraham or even Noah?
   ___Don't You think some of the disciples felt left out when they didn't have this particular "mountaintop experience"?
   ___Are these "mountaintop experiences" really helpful to people later?

C. When I think of my own life in terms of high points and low points, I see my life as
   ___all mountains, no valleys!
   ___all valleys, no mountains!
   ___mostly valleys, with an occasional mountain!
   ___mostly mountains, with a valley or two from time to time!

D. If another mountaintop experience were to occur in my life, it would most likely take place
   ___when I'm with a group of close friends;
   ___in my family circle;
   ___when I'm with a certain group of kids from church;
   ___in a worship service; or
   ___with one special friend from school.

E. God directed a word or two to Peter, James, and John. He spoke out of that bright cloud, "This is My own dear Son, with whom I am well pleased—listen to Him!" Without question, those words were directed to the three disciples, because God knew those were the words they needed for faith and life at that moment.

Knowing the mountains and valleys that exist in your life, what do you think your heavenly Father would say to you? Would His words be words of direction, encouragement, support, hope, or even forgiveness? Write a statement as you think God would speak to you at this moment in your life.

After each person has finished writing, ask the small groups of four to six to begin sharing individually within their groups what members have written, i.e., ask each person, in turn, to share his or her response to A as he or she wishes. Then move to B and repeat the procedure. Move through each of the five statements in the same way.

Worship

Scripture Reading: 2 Peter 1:16–19

Devotional Thoughts in Response

Peter looks back to that mountaintop experience and connects it to his whole life. There was purpose for him in that event on the mountain. For Peter, it was a matter of being able to say, "I'm not talking about a Lord Jesus from secondhand experience. I was there! I saw Him! I heard the voice! I saw the glory of God!"

The impact of that experience stayed with Peter and supported him throughout his life.

Think back on some of the experiences that you thought about and talked about this evening. Some of those were mountaintop experiences—some were valleys. These experiences affect you now and will continue to have an impact on your lives. In faith we know that the result of an event—even a bad one—can be for our good. From Rom. 8:28 come these words: "We know that in all things God works for good with those who love Him, those whom He has called according to His purpose."

Litany

Group 1: O Lord Jesus Christ, we place our lives before You.
Group 2: You know so well each mountain and valley we experience.
Group 1: For the joy of each "mountaintop,"
Group 2: we thank You. You give really great gifts!
Group 1: In the presence of valleys that are all too real and all too painful,
Group 2: we look to You for help, for support, and for hope.
Group 1: From allowing mountaintops to mislead us into a false sense of trust in ourselves,
Group 2: O Lord, deliver us.
Group 1: From seeing low points only as proof that we are consistent failures,
Group 2: O Lord, protect us.
Group 1: In the middle of mountains and valleys,
Group 2: Assure us of Your presence and power.
Group 1: Through the mountains and valleys, which are certain to occur in our lives,
Group 2: lead us to an even greater dependence on Your Word and Your will for our lives.

Hymn

"Shout from the Highest Mountain"

Recreation (30 min.)

Mountaintop (Building) Experience

There are two variations to this game: Ten-Member Pyramids and Big Rock Candy Mountain. To play Ten-Member Pyramids, ask four sturdily built people to kneel side-by-side for the base of the pyramid. Put three medium-sized people who don't mind being in the middle of the thing on the second row.

The New Games Book describes a people pyramid it calls the Big Rock Candy Mountain. This pyramid is circular in style and can involve 15 to 25 people. You can use as many as 10 to 12 of the sturdy type for the bottom of this architectural masterpiece.

Form that bottom "row" in a circle.

Then build up succeeding rows, always following the circle pattern, until that one courageous person ascends the top.

It is a good idea to use a couple of spotters to help support and catch falling bodies.

You may wish to use both styles of pyramids for variety. Or you may prefer to pick the style that best suits your group. In any event, building the pyramid will trigger some comments about mountaintop experiences. You may even hear someone on the bottom row murmuring something about a valley or two!

How to Keep the Mountain from Crashing into the Valley

You may know this game by its more familiar title, "Pass the Bod."

Have 10 to 12 participants form a circle, sitting on the floor—shoes off. One brave (and usually lightweight) person stands in the middle of that circle. All members of the circle extend their feet to the center, "looking in," the single person standing in the middle. Members of that circle, sitting with their feet extended toward the middle of the circle, now extend their arms out and up. The person in the middle is to stiffen himself or herself, cross arms over chest, and trustingly lean backward to be caught and supported by the outstretched arms of those in the circle. The circle then "passes the bod" around, attempting to move that "bod" as rapidly as possible without letting that "bod" fall on the members of the circle. (That's definitely a "valley type" experience.)

Try several different people in the middle. If you have a large group, have several circles of 10 to 12 going on at the same time. Expect some insightful comments about being down in the valley from some of those in the circle. Some of those brave people in the middle who get "passed around" might even mention something about the dizzying mountaintop experience of flying around the circle.

The Afterglow—Refreshments and Fellowship

Give refreshments special names that tie in with the mountain and valley theme. Let your imagination run wild. Potato chips could suddenly become "mountaintop taters." Even ordinary popcorn could be renamed "topper poppers." Some parts of the country have a mountain-valley brand of soft drink! See what you can do with creative renaming of ordinary things.

Informal fellowship to end an evening "slowly" can be very important. This is an excellent time to make use of some of the youth group members that play guitars. A sing along is great to wind down activities.

If no guitar talent is available, records (some of them the sing-along type) might provide good background music. This should be a "come and go" time with kids leaving, meeting rides, and such. It can also be a great time for counselors and leaders to be available for those brief chats with kids.

Behind the Wheel

by Kurt Bickel

Objective

To explore the decisions of the Christian teenager behind the wheel

Materials Needed

    Old magazines
    Scissors
    Glue
    Construction paper
    Roleplay cards
    String or yarn
    Magic marker or crayon
    Printed copies of Accessory List
    Bibles
    Five or more clippings of auto accidents

Introduction to Topic

When a teenager gets behind the wheel of an automobile, conflicting feelings invade his or her thinking. The driver's seat represents privilege, liberty, freedom, and individualism. On the one hand the youth feels "in control"; and on the other, the constraint of society to be an adult. Dr. Charlie W. Shedd says, "Do you know, Mom and Dad, that the day your kid gets his driver's license is a whole lot holier to him than the day he was baptized? You don't think so? Come on—come alive, it is!"

In contrast to this feeling of licensed privilege comes that of obligation, liability, and responsibility.

This youth meeting explores the decisions of the Christian teenager behind the wheel through the following activities:

    Icebreaker: Motoring Name Tags (15 min.)
    Continuum: Where Do You Stand? (15 min.)
    Roleplay and Bible Discussion: (45 min.)
        Wheels of My Own
        All in the Family
        Cruising
    Recreation: Traffic Jam Game (15 min.)
    Worship: Psalms for the Road (10 min.)
    Afterglow: Travel to a Home or Restaurant (20 min.)

Icebreaker: Motoring Name Tags

As the youth arrive, have them each make a motoring name tag. You might have yours made in advance as a sample. Give the youth the directions below.

1. Write your name at the top of the paper.
2. From a magazine cut out a car that reflects your personality. Glue it in the center of the paper.
3. Give yourself a CB handle and write it in the lower right corner of the paper.
4. Choose three accessories from the list and write down what they are in the lower left.

List of Accessories

    Air conditioner: I need to control my hot temper.
    CB radio: I like to talk.
    Litter bag: A clean environment is important to me.
    Dual sport mirrors: I was happier in the past than I am now.
    Cruise control: I like to take life at a steady pace.
    Adjustable steering wheel: I like change in my life.
    Reclining seats: I like to take life easy.
    Visor mirror: Personal appearance is important to me.
    Swivel seat: I'm always ready to jump into action.
    Extra duty shocks: When I get put down, I spring back quickly.
    Dual exhaust: I'm not afraid to speak out on my views.

When everyone has completed making the tags, have each person explain his or her tag to the group. You can do this in small groups or with the entire group together in a casual party style.

Continuum—Where Do You Stand?

In this activity group members will show where they stand on issues concerning the automobile. Make seven markers of plain paper to lay on the floor in a straight line across the room. The markers should read in order: +++, ++, +, 0, -, --, ---. Explain that you will read a statement and that group members should stand by the marker that reflects their opinion, +++ being strongly agree and --- strongly disagree. You may wish to conduct a brief discussion after each statement.

The "Where Do You Stand?" statements are as follows:

1. You should never pick up hitchhikers.
2. A car is a reflection of the owner's personality.
3. The 55-miles per hour speed limit should be lifted.
4. It's unfair for insurance companies to charge more for boys than girls.
5. Driver education class is more important than confirmation class.
6. Motorcyclists should be able to ride with or without helmets.
7. There should be stiffer penalties for driving while drunk.
8. Boys can't really start dating until they have their driver's license.
9. It's a good idea for insurance rates to be cheaper for students with good grades.

10. The Bible doesn't speak about auto safety.
11. Most kids drive wildly to show off.
12. Parents do not have the right to regulate with whom you ride.
13. CB radios contribute more to highway hazard than highway safety.
14. Girls tend to date the guys with nicer cars.
15. Parents have the right to check your odometer.
16. Police stop teenagers more than other motorists.
17. Teenagers make better drivers than any other age group.
18. The time is coming when there will be no personal transportation.

Roleplay and Bible Discussion

Materials Needed: Roleplay Cards and Bibles

Below are three roleplay situations. Choose volunteers to act out the role in front of the group. In preparation the volunteers should read only their cards. Instruct the roleplayers to play the role as if they were that person. Stop the roleplay when it slows down or becomes repetitious. It is not necessary that the players resolve the problem. After each roleplay is completed, ask the group to discuss the following questions:

1. What's the problem(s) in this roleplay?
2. Is it a real life situation? Why or why not?
3. How would you solve the problem?
4. Does our Christian faith help us find a solution for this situation?
5. How are the passages printed after each roleplay helpful?

Roleplay 1: "Wheels of My Own"

Characters: Bill, Dad, Mom

Bill—You are 17 years old, and you want to buy a car of your own. You have saved up half the money for a "vintage Mustang." You have to ask your dad to cosign for the loan. You are afraid he will say no. Your reasons for getting the car: You could get a job after school to pay off the loan. You wouldn't have to bother your parents for rides anymore. You would have greater independence. You would take better care of your own car. The family station wagon doesn't make it with the girls.

Dad—Your son, Bill, 17, asks you to cosign for a car, but you are afraid of all the costs. You ask a lot of questions: Why can't you drive my station wagon? How much does the car cost? Who will pay for the gas? How do you expect to pay off the loan? Do you realize how high insurance will be? And on and on . . .

Mom—Your 17-year-old son, Bill, wants to buy a car of his own. Bill has been out with friends a lot lately, and his grades are slipping. You feel that if he has his own car it will make matters worse. You think the car would offer too much freedom. With the family station wagon you could have more control over what he does. If he gets his own car, you are afraid of all kinds of problems: bad friends, booze, drugs, and skipping school.

Bible References for "Wheels of My Own"

Phil. 2:1-15   Col. 3:5-17

Roleplay 2: "All in the Family"

Characters: Mom, Dad, Bud, and Sis

Dad—You have only one car, and it seems you never get to use it. Just once in a while you would like to take a drive in the country or go fishing on the weekends. Yet it seems someone always has the car. You feel cheated because you make the payments and pay the higher insurance rates for teenaged drivers. Many times when you have to be somewhere there is no gas in the car. You would like another car but can't afford it.

Mom—You feel as if all you do is provide taxi service for everyone, and you resent it. You take Dad to work and the kids to school. You have to pick up everyone again, and sometimes there are after school meetings. The schedules are always changing, so you have to plan each day differently. You would love to have a second car, but you just can't afford it.

Bud—You just got your license, and it seems like you never get to drive the car, except for an occasional short errand. Sis gets to take it to all her evening school events. She had it for the last three weekends. You promised not to tell, but you know she skipped the last church youth meeting and went driving around with a group of girlfriends instead.

Sis—You need the car a lot for school activities. You're the only one of your friends who has her driver's license. Your dad usually lets you have the car, but he always puts up a big fuss, hollers a lot, and gives you a long lecture. Because he gets so upset, you're becoming afraid to ask him for the car. Instead of going through the hassle, you've been staying home, and you don't like it.

Bible References for "All in the Family"

Eph. 5:21; 6:4   1 John 4:7-12

Roleplay 3: "Cruising"

Characters: Speed, Sue, Ann, Ralph

Speed—You just got a new car. You shined it up and filled the gas tank in preparation for a night of cruising all the hangouts. You decide to take some friends along: Ralph, Ann, and Sue. You want to show them what your new car will do, so you drive it hard and fast. Your friends start asking you to slow down, but you think they must be kidding, so you keep going faster. You won't slow down no matter what.

Sue—You are riding with your friends in Speed's new car. You love to go cruising. The faster the better. You keep encouraging Speed to drive faster even when the others start getting scared. You think they are a bunch of chickens.

Ralph—You and your friends Ann and Sue go for a ride in Speed's new car. Speed is driving too fast and wild. You are becoming afraid, but you don't want to admit it, until Ann says she is scared. You try to keep your cool, but you really want Speed to stop his crazy driving.

Ann—You are out for a ride with your friends, but Speed keeps driving faster and faster. You become afraid and uncomfortable. You tell Speed to please slow down. He doesn't listen. You tell him that if he doesn't slow down, you're getting out. You tell him that a cousin of yours was killed last week in a car wreck, and you're afraid. If he still doesn't slow down, you demand that he take you home.

Bible References for "Cruising"

Ps. 1:1   Gal. 5:16-24

Recreation: Traffic Jam*

Necessities: 8-10 players
1 traffic cop (appoint someone)
a string of squares (marked on the ground with tape, chalk, or paper), numbering one more than the number of people in the group

Task: Group 1 and Group 2 are to exchange places in the squares—a human version of an old Eastern Puzzle.

Parameters: Set up the squares about an easy step apart in distance, with the groups arranged as shown. It can be done:

Group 1   → → → → → ☐ ← ← ← ← ←   Group 2

Legal Moves:

A person can move
into an empty space
in front of him/her.

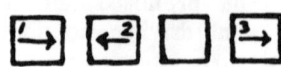

Legal for 1 or 2

A person can move
around a person who
is facing him/her.

Legal for 1 or more

Illegal Moves:

Backward
Around someone facing the same way
Two people moving at the same time

Worship and Afterglow

You may stay in the same setting and do the following worship, or you might take a ride in cars as part of the "Behind the Wheel" experience. Or drive to a restaurant for an afterglow fellowship.

Another option would be to go to a member's house for refreshments and worship. Passengers in each car could prepare a prayer and praise psalm as they travel.

Psalms for the Road

Before the meeting collect at least five newspaper clippings of auto accidents. Distribute them to members of the group.

Alternate reading a clipping and the psalms in the order shown below:

Ps. 5:11-12
Ps. 10:12-14
Ps. 32:7-9
Ps. 16:1
Ps. 36:5-7

If any of the young people had friends or family involved in an auto accident, talk about it and pray about it.

*Taken from 1976 Kaleidoscope Staff Manual, Board for Youth Services, The Lutheran Church—Missouri Synod. Used by permission.

Decisions Involving Jobs

by Steve Sonnenberg

Objective

To explore values that must be taken into account in job-related decisions

Materials Needed

Construction paper
Art scraps
Glue, tape, stapler

Paper and pencils for each person
Personal qualifications list
Newsprint and marker or blackboard
Five index cards or self-sticking name tags for each person
A sheet of paper large enough to accommodate all the index cards in a cross formation.

Opening Activity: Job Hats

Arrange a table (or other area) with an ample supply of colored paper, tape, glue, staples, and other art scraps to make hats for everyone who attends the meeting. As the youth arrive, send them to the table with instructions to make a hat that will represent some kind of job. It could be the job they now have, what they thought they wanted to be when they grew up, their parent's job, or any other job that appeals to them. Ask them to avoid telling anyone else what occupation is represented by their hat. Encourage decorating the hats in ways that help depict some of the services provided by that vocation. When the hats are completed, ask their respective designers to wear them throughout the evening.

After each participant has had ample opportunity to make and model a hat, ask him or her to be seated. Hand out paper and pencils with the following instructions: Write an ad to advertise a desire to hire someone to fill the position represented by the hat you are wearing. Your ad should be concise, descriptive of the skill needed, and the performance expectations. *DO NOT name the job in your ad.* Merely describe it well enough so that anyone reading the ad would know if he or she is qualified for the job.

When everyone has completed his or her ad, go around the group, showing each hat and reading each ad. The rest of the group should try to guess the job being described. (15 min.)

Listing Job Skills

Solicit examples of criteria or qualifications necessary for the various jobs described and write these ideas on newsprint or chalkboard. Search for words that refer to characteristics that apply in a general way to almost any job, for example, honesty, dependability, punctuality, persistence, independence, kindness or warmth, cooperative attitude, and concern for others. If necessary, ask the group to try to think of these more general skills or attributes. Post this list where it will be visible throughout the meeting. (5 min.)

Prioritizing Job Qualifications

Give each person a prepared list of personal qualifications with the following instructions: Rank these criteria in *order of importance for any job*. The most important thing should be numbered 1, the second most important 2, and so forth, all the way to the least important, which is 10. Mark your number in column B.

A	B	
__	__	Is willing to work for low pay to start
__	__	Has never been in trouble with the law
__	__	Gets along well with people
__	__	Needs the money
__	__	Is honest and trustworthy
__	__	Has previous experience
__	__	Is pretty smart/catches on fast
__	__	Is punctual (comes to work on time)
__	__	Is planning to work there for a year or more
__	__	Works as hard when the boss is gone as when he/she is there

Give each person about three minutes to rank his or her list; then form groups of four to compare lists. Each foursome should rerank the items using column A to record their corporate ranking. The only rule is that all four members of the small group must agree on the ranking. Share the results of the small group rankings with the whole group. Allow at least five minutes for discussion of this experience. (20 min.)

Ethical Decisions at Work

This activity is designed to give the participants an opportunity to take a stand on many of the decisions that may be a part of everyday work. It will provide a chance to check out how their decisions compare with the decisions of many of their peers.

Clear an area of the room and mark a row of five spots on the floor. This can be done by laying five pieces of paper on the floor. The paper on one end of the line should read "Strongly Agree"; the next piece should read "Agree"; the middle piece "Just don't know"; the fourth reads "Disagree"; and the last one reads "Strongly Disagree."

Explain that you will read a statement and ask the group members to position themselves near the paper on the floor that best expresses their feelings. Read the first statement. Have the players position themselves and look around to see who is standing where. Pause for a few minutes of discussion about the issue just voted on. Then read the next statement and continue the process. (20 min.)

Job Decision Poll Questions

1. Most young people work at a job because it's fun.
2. When you see a fellow employee breaking a work rule, it's part of your responsibility to report it.
3. It is all right to take things from work as long as they are not worth too much!
4. The amount of pay received for a particular job isn't really all that important if you enjoy the work.
5. It's all right to show some emotion at work, such as crying, shouting, or laughing a lot.
6. It's a good idea for companies to require their employees to wear specific uniforms.
7. Whether or not a job interferes with church participation is not really very important.
8. It doesn't really matter *how* I get a job, just so I get it.
9. It's all right to lie about your qualifications for a job if you're sure you can do the work and really want a chance.
10. It would be better to be paid for the amount of work you do than just for the number of hours you put in.
11. It is all right to use drugs or alcohol while at work, so long as no one knows, and you can still get the job done.
12. You should stay with a good job even though you feel like a failure or are bored with it.

Worship (10 min.)

Give each person five 3" x 5" index cards (or self-sticking name tags). Ask participants to write on each card one thing they can do well and should get paid for. Or have them write down some talent or skill they could bring to a job. Fasten the cards in the shape of a cross to a large sheet of colored paper that was hung on the wall before the meeting began. Use Christmas paper, wallpaper, or construction paper (or something like it) large enough to accommodate five cards from each participant.

1. Read some of the talents, skills, and gifts that the people have posted in the cross form.
2. Prayer: *Lord, we ask that You bless these talents and skills. Bless the people to whom they belong. Help to provide opportunities for the use of them in Your kingdom. Amen.*
3. Read Ps. 8.
4. Pray the following litany for the use of our skills.
    Leader: We acknowledge that the skills and talents we have are gifts that You, O Lord, have given us.
    Group: Bless us, Lord; guide us, Lord!
    Leader: These precious gifts have been entrusted to us for service to You and Your world. We accept that challenge and will do our best with them.
    Group: Bless us, Lord; guide us, Lord.
    Leader: Show us the ways that You can best be served by our talents.
    Group: Bless us, Lord; guide us, Lord.
    Leader: Open opportunities for us to use these skills. Help us find jobs where the talent we have can be put into service for You.
    Group: Bless us, Lord; guide us, Lord.

Leader: Be with us when we must make decisions about whether to get a job, how to get work, and what we will do with our money; help us to be laborers worthy of our hire.
Group: Bless us, Lord; guide us, Lord.
Leader: The many gifts You have given are for us to use. Help us to develop and commit them to Your service.
Group: Bless us, Lord; guide us, Lord.

Conclude the worship by singing songs of celebration for talents and skills, for instance:
"They Will Know We Are Christians by Our Love"
"Give Us a Song"
"Thank You"
"What So Ever You Do"

The meeting could conclude with refreshments.

Optional Activities

The following are optional or continuing ways to use this theme:
1. Establish a "placement/employment" service in your newsletter or on a bulletin board.
2. Create a volunteer service: NEED HELP will provide help.
3. Sponsor a "vocational night," featuring members of the congregation who will talk about their jobs.
4. Have someone write about "the perfect working situation."

Let's Be Friends
(Nondating Relationships)

by Alan Gunderman

Objectives

That the youth become more sensitive to each others' concerns, feelings, difficulties, and successes as they struggle in friendship with members of the other sex

That the youth begin to understand the need for intimacy and, by the grace of God, be better equipped to make wise decisions in fulfilling that need

That the youth have opportunity to share their attitudes and feelings about friendships with the other sex

That the youth might strengthen friendships that already exist and give thanks and praise to God for the gift of friendship

Materials Needed

Survey form for each participant
Chalkboard or flipchart
Pencils
8 1/2" x 11" paper
Bibles

Getting Started (20 min.)

1. As each teenager arrives, give him or her a "Nondating—Opposite Sex—Friendship Survey" form to be filled out quickly and privately.
2. While the teenagers are involved in items 3 and 4, have one counselor tally the results of the "Nondating—Opposite Sex—Friendship Survey" form on a chalkboard or large flip chart

in the following manner:

		Female Responses			Male Responses		
		1	2	3	1	2	3
Statements on Friendship	1						
	2						
	3						
	4						
	5						
	6						
	7						
	8						
	9						
	10						

3. As each person finishes the survey, have the youth gather in groups of four, with an even distribution of males and females, if possible.
4. Give the following instructions to each group, or post them where everyone can see them. Make sure there are enough pencils and paper for everyone.
   a. Introduce yourselves to each other. If you don't know each other very well, spend another minute sharing your age, your school, and one interest.
   b. Choose someone to be the group "starter." The starters should make sure each person has a chance to speak.
   c. Using an 8 1/2" x 11" piece of paper, write your name or nickname, each letter in order, down the left side of your paper. Choose words or short phrases that begin with those letters of your name to describe what kind of friend you are. Let's call this our Friendship Acronym.

   Example: A—Admiring
   L—Lovable
   A—Always selective
   N—Not negative

   d. When the group is ready, each person should share his or her Friendship Acronym with the rest. If you feel like you know each other well enough, suggest other words that would fit in each other's Friendship Acronym.
   e. If time permits, take turns doing the following: three members of the group should share with the remaining one those words that best describe that person as a friend.

Learning Experience

A. In your group answer the following questions. Assign someone the responsibility of recording your group's answers. The "starter" is to make sure the discussion keeps flowing and that everyone has a chance to share. Check your group responses with the composite response given on the Friendship Survey Form. (20 min.)
   1. Is it difficult to maintain a nondating friendship with a member of the opposite sex? If so, why?
   2. Is it more difficult for males or females to initiate and maintain a friendship with a member of the opposite sex? Why?

3. How do you think our culture has affected nondating male-female relationships?
4. When you marry, how do you think you will feel if your spouse has a close friend of the opposite sex? Do you think it's a good idea to have such friends? Why or why not?
5. Look up 1 John 1:8—2:2 and 1 John 2:9–12 for some "light" from God's Word. What does it mean to live in the "light" as described in verse 10 of chapter 2? Do verses 8 and 9 of chapter 1 and verses 1 and 2 of chapter 2 help us answer the previous question? Is friendship earned or is it a gift?

Take time now for each group to share significant answers with the whole group. Special note should be made of the correlation between the small group answers and the composite responses to the Friendship Survey Form. (10 min.)

B. If there is time to make the event last 30 minutes longer, discuss the following statements in groups of four or as a larger group. State whether you agree or disagree and tell why. Perhaps you could spend time suggesting ways each situation could be remedied. (30 min.)

1. American teenagers worry too much and too early about dating relationships. They ought to be spending their time and energy developing friendships.
2. A tragedy in the American dating scene is that often teenagers can communicate more freely and intimately with a member of the opposite sex they are not dating than they can with the person whom they are dating. As a result they end up marrying the wrong person.
3. Teenagers tend to look for intimacy in sexual activity instead of in a more satisfying emotional area.
4. Teenagers need to learn that emotional intimacy can be helpful, satisfying, and rewarding without sexual intimacy. Sexual intimacy is always best when connected with emotional intimacy.

Worship (10–15 min.)

Sing: "You've Got a Friend" by Carole King or some other song concerning friendship. (The song can be introduced by stating that these could be Jesus' words to us.)

Scripture: Eph. 4:25–32

This should be read by a good reader in the group. Then allow for thoughts or reactions from the group. Don't be afraid of silence.

Prayer: The following prayer is divided into two parts. The first half is a confession of sins. After each line is shared by the leader, group members are to respond, "forgive me, Lord." The leader may want to invite group members to share confessional statements of their own with everyone responding, "forgive me, Lord."

The second half is a thanksgiving service. After each line is shared by the leader, the group is to respond, "thank You, Lord, for Your grace." The leader should remind everyone that grace is undeserved love. Again, the leader may want to invite group members to share thanksgiving statements of their own with everyone responding, "thank You, Lord, for Your grace."

Leave a period of silence after each section of the prayer. Let us pray:

L: When I am not a friend to someone who desperately needs a friend . . .
R: forgive me, Lord.
L: When I choose friendships for what I can get out of them instead of what I can give to them . . .
R: forgive me, Lord.
L: When I allow the people and culture around me to have too great an influence in the choosing of my friends . . .
R: forgive me, Lord.
L: When I am not a listening friend . . .
R: forgive me, Lord.
L: When I betray intimacies with friends at their expense . . .
R: forgive me, Lord.
L: When I bring darkness instead of light into the lives of my friends . . .
R: forgive me, Lord.
  (Silence)
L: For friends who are dependable, trustworthy, and sure . . .

R: thank You, Lord, for Your grace.
L: For friends who love me even when I am not very lovable . . .
R: thank You, Lord, for Your grace.
L: For friends who bring light when my life seems to be filled with darkness . . .
R: thank You, Lord, for Your grace.
L: For forgiving me so I can forgive my friends . . .
R: thank You, Lord, for Your grace.
L: For giving us Your Son, Jesus, as our most faithful Friend . . .
R: thank You, Lord, for Your grace.
(Silence)

End by praying the Lord's Prayer together.
Sing: "I Am the Light of the World" by Jim Strathdee

Haiku Writing

Distribute pencils, pens, and paper to the group. Bring along the dictionary definition of haiku and some examples. Ask each student to write one haiku concerning friendship. The haiku can be about one certain person or experience, or it can be a general description of what friendship means. Have each person sign his or her poem, but instruct each of them not to share yet.

When everyone has finished, collect all the poems and read them without identifying the authors. Then have the group vote for first, second, and third award prizes for the haikus that best express friendship. After the vote, ask the authors to identify themselves. Then read all the poems again, one by one, returning them to their authors as you finish.

Wink'em

This game works best when the male-female ratio is about even. Perhaps a few volunteers could take on the role of the opposite sex in order to make the game work.

1. All the members of one sex sit on chairs in a rather loose circle. Each member of the opposite sex is to stand behind one of the occupied chairs, with hands behind his or her back and eyes looking directly down on the person's head in front. One person stands behind an empty chair and starts the game (e.g., if you have 10 boys and 11 girls, the 10 boys sit with one of the girls standing behind each. The 11th girl stands behind an empty chair).
2. The person with the empty chair is to fill his or her chair by winking at one of the sitting persons. The person winked at is to move as quickly as possible to the empty chair.
3. When a person standing notices the person in his or her chair starting to move, he or she grabs the shoulders of that person and holds the person back to keep the chair filled.
4. Each person standing starts with his or her head down and hands behind his or her back. Each person sitting starts with his or her back flat against the chair. A person must remain in the chair if the person behind him or her touches each shoulder.
5. Approximately halfway through the game, those standing switch places with those sitting. Counselors, too, can play.

Refreshments

While they are enjoying refreshments, ask participants to discuss what they enjoyed most that night with someone whom they learned more about that evening.

Nondating—Opposite Sex—Friendship Survey

Before you respond to the statements, read these definitions:

Friend—A person with whom one enjoys spending time. A person with whom one shares "things" about oneself that are not shared with just anyone. One does not usually have more than two or three good friends. (For our purposes here, let us rule out family members.)

Sexual Intimacy—The sharing of one's body with another person. It can range from hand holding, kissing, and necking to heavy petting and sexual intercourse.

Emotional Intimacy—The sharing of very personal thoughts and feelings with another person.

Please respond to the 10 statements with 1, 2, or 3.

Number 1 signifies agreement—This doesn't have to be total agreement but more agreement than disagreement.

Number 2 signifies disagreement—This doesn't have to be total disagreement but more disagreement than agreement.

Number 3 signifies "can't answer"—This is reserved for the times when the question is not applicable to you or when you *really* can't decide one way or the other. Try to avoid using this one.

Please return this form to your leader when you are finished.

___Male   ___Female   (Check one)

___ 1. I have a friend (by the above definition) of the opposite sex whom I am not dating.
___ 2. I am (would be) perfectly comfortable having a friendship with a member of the opposite sex, even though I am quite sure it will never be a dating relationship.
___ 3. I feel it is easier for females than it is for males to develop nondating friendships with members of the opposite sex.
___ 4. I feel it is easier for males than it is for females to develop nondating friendships with members of the opposite sex.
___ 5. There have been times when I have wanted a nondating friendship with a member of the opposite sex but have held back because I was afraid it might be misunderstood as a desire for a dating relationship.
___ 6. I won't waste my time trying to develop a friendship with a member of the opposite sex if dating is not a possibility.
___ 7. Whenever I have a friend of the opposite sex, I often feel pressure for it to become a dating relationship.
___ 8. It is (would be) easy for me to accept the fact that the person I am dating has a close friend who is the same sex as I.
___ 9. I am often more comfortable in sharing my thoughts and feelings with a nondating friend of the opposite sex than I am with the person I am dating.
___ 10. It is easier to be emotionally intimate than it is to be sexually intimate with a member of the opposite sex.

My Body—My Buddy
(My Sexuality)

by Steve Sonnenberg

Objectives

To provide an opportunity for participants to discover or rediscover the best parts of their bodies
To create a setting in which participants can reinforce each other's good feelings about their bodies
To look at Bible passages that refer to bodies

Materials Needed

About 10 sheets of newsprint and markers (or chalkboard and chalk)
Old magazines or newspapers
2 sheets of 8-1/2" x 11" paper per person
Pencils
Glue and masking tape or pins
Bibles
Several frisbees or paper plates
Large sheet of paper (optional)

Introduction to Topic

Name something either:
>too big or too small,
>too short or too tall,
>too broad or too lean,
>too far in between,
>too dark or too light,
>but never just right!

Answer: A person's body!

Have you ever met anyone who was completely satisfied with his or her body? Hundreds of gimmicks, such as cosmetics, clothes, food supplements, diets, exercise programs, consultation services, plastic surgeons, and contact lenses, are aimed at adjusting one's appearance. These are all things to help people look better or to make them feel they look better.

This gathering is designed to help group members discover and accept at least one (or more) parts of their body as a "good gift from God."

Opening Activities (10 min.)

Before the participants arrive, print and display the "Name something . . ." riddle (at the beginning of this topic) on a large sheet of newsprint or chalkboard. Have magic markers or pieces of chalk handy for people to write their anwers to the puzzle on the riddle sheet. (It may take some prodding to get things going.) Save the answer for later!

As people arrive, ask them to look through old magazines or newspapers to find one or several advertisements that remind them of their bodies. Have them clip the ads, write their names on them, and tape or pin the ads to the wall somewhere in the meeting room. Small ads could be glued to an 8 1/2" x 11" sheet of paper before hanging them.

Begin the session by having each person explain how one of his or her ads fits his or her body. If the chosen ad and accompanying explanation are predominantly positive, mark the picture with a + (plus). If they are negative, mark it with a – (minus). Note with the group whether most of the pictures represent positive or negative characteristics. Discuss for a moment what this observation says about self-image. Do members of the group feel good about their bodies? Why or why not?

Bible Study (20 min.)

After discussing personal feelings about one's body, ask each person to look at 1 Cor. 3:16–17. Someone could read this section out loud while the others follow along.

A prayer similar to the following could be used after the reading of the verses:

Dear Lord,

Listen, please, to the words and thoughts of Your creatures. The body You have given each of us is the dwelling place of the Spirit. Help us to believe that what we are, what we look like, and what we are capable of are all part of Your plan for us. Guide us in the exploration of our body as Your temple—Your gift to us—and our gift to You.

Send Your Spirit into the heart of each of us here. Use Your Word to help us discover how we can use our bodies for Your service. Thank You. Amen.

On a piece of newsprint or the chalkboard list examples of how a temple can fulfill the function of

strength	example in the community
honoring God	worshiping God
being God's dwelling place	

Make another list. This time write examples of how a person's body can fulfill the function of

strength	example in the community
honoring God	worshiping God
being God's dwelling place	

Compare the two lists and discuss the many ways in which our bodies are similar to God's temple. What are some ideas Paul is referring to when he says, "You are the temple [house] of the Lord"?

Divide into small groups of four or six people and read 1 Cor. 6:19–20. Write the words "home," "gift," "loan," "purchase," and "obligation" separately at the top of sheets of newsprint and post them on the wall (or write the words across the top of the chalkboard). Direct each small group to discuss how a person's attitude toward his or her body might be influenced by knowing that it is a home, gift, loan, purchase, or obligation. The groups could make their own list, or simply remember the discussion, to share discoveries with the whole group later.

After the small groups have completed this task, ask each one to share its discoveries with the group at large. The leader should make notes of the reports on the appropriate newsprint sheet or beneath the correct word on the chalkboard.

Group Activity (20 min.)

God's Word says that He made our bodies in His image as a dwelling place for His Spirit. You've probably seen or heard the slogan "God don't make no junk" or "Please be patient—God isn't finished with me yet." We are all His creation made to serve Him. Even knowing that, we don't always feel good about the shape, appearance, or capacity of the bodies He gave us. The next activities are designed to promote positive, affirming feelings about each person's own body. *A word of caution to the leader:* Talking about one's own body can be very threatening. Handle the discussion gently. If necessary, encourage group members to take the exercises seriously and with as positive an attitude as they can.

The first exercise is intended to help group members actively think about their bodies. Clear a space so that the participants can form a single-file line across the center of the room. Suggest that there is an imaginary line on the floor representing varying points of view. Divide this imaginary line into five equal lengths by placing a piece of tape or a chalk mark on the floor to represent options. The far left section of the line should represent the response, "I like it very much" (I.L.I.V.M.); next, "I like it" (I.L.I.); the middle position represents "It really doesn't matter" (I.R.D.M.); the next position stands for "I dislike it" (I.D.I.); and the far right end represents "I dislike it very much" (I.D.I.V.M.). Thus the line will be divided as follows:

(I.L.I.V.M.)   (I.L.I.)   (I.R.D.M.)   (I.D.I.)   (I.D.I.V.M.)

Ask the youth to close their eyes and visualize their own body. The leader should call out a specific body part. Participants should visualize their own anatomy—then open their eyes and move to the spot on the line that represents their feelings about that part of their body. See who else is standing in that spot with you. Then continue with other body words. Body words that might be used (feel free to add or subtract from this list) include

hair	legs	calves	eyes	chin
mouth	ears	back	thighs	smile
knees	ankles	hands	chest	toes
shoulders	stomach	feet	finger nails	hips
neck	nose	rear	face	throat
cheeks	teeth	arms	tongue	elbows

The second activity is designed to help each participant think positively about some of his or her own body parts and give affirmations to each other. Give each individual a piece of paper and a pencil. Introduce the experience with these words: "A team of scientists have been given the task of designing the 'perfect human being.' You were selected as the model for three body parts to be used in the 'perfect being.' Which three parts of you are the ones they will use? Write these words on your piece of paper and fold it in half."

Form groups of four to six people again. Pretend the other people in the small group are the scientists. They will tell you which three parts of you will be used, and why. Don't tell them the choices you have written on your paper. Just listen as the others suggest and discuss your best features. When the team has made its choice, the "model" should reveal his or her own words on the folded sheet of paper. Allow some time for the model and the team to share their common and different choices. Why is everyone's opinion so different? Continue around the small group, giving each person an opportunity to be the "model."

Recreation (20 min.)

The first game helps establish an awareness of one's body by having participants avoid contact with each other. The second game depends upon touching each other. Both are variations of games described in *The New Game Book*.

Grab a Disc

Lay a few frisbees on the ground (if out-of-doors) or paper plates on the floor, estimating one disc per 10 or 12 people. Have group members walk around the discs, humming or clapping until the leader yells, "Grab!" Everyone must scramble to touch one of the discs. The last person to reach a disc is "out." If any two or more people touch each other in the process of getting to a disc, they are all "out." When the number of players still "in" gets smaller, remove one disc to keep competition keen. Notice a person's body awareness when the objective is to prevent contact of any type.

Hug Tag

This game is played much like other games of tag. One person, "it," must run after others in the group and try to touch someone in order to make that person "it." The special variation of this game allows for a potential "it" to be "safe" if he or she is hugging or holding on to someone else when tagged. To walk around holding hands or carrying each other from spot to spot is unfair. Some exciting game variations could include a rule that only three people hugging are safe. How about a foursome or fivesome? Notice the freedom to put bodies together in a fun way.

After both games have been completed, sit down with the entire group to discuss the feelings each person had when playing them. Ask the players which game they liked better, the game that prohibited touching or the one that promoted it? Why?

If you haven't already done so—be sure to identify the answer to the "Name Something Riddle."

Devotion (15 min.)

Have somone lie on a large sheet of paper. Draw or trace around the person to get an outline of his or her body. Tape this silhouette to the wall or lay it on the floor in the center of the circle of participants.

Begin the worship by reading Ps. 139:13–17. While group members meditate on what it means to be God's creation, have each one write his or her name on the silhouette at the spot the committee of "scientists" determined was their best feature. (Probably several names will be in the same places.)

Continue with a song, such as "We Are One in the Spirit," "Just a Closer Walk with Thee," "Them Bones, Them Dry Bones," "Here Comes Jesus," or "Whole Earth, Whole People."

Conclude the worship with a circle prayer. Each participant should follow this format: "I thank You, Lord, for (list the body parts you and your "scientists" selected as "perfect model" parts). They are truly gifts from You. Help me to use them in Your service." When everyone has finished his or her prayer, close the worship by asking God's blessing for all the bodies present.

Refreshments (5 min.)

Conclude the meeting with "health food" refreshments like fruit, nuts, raisins, natural cereals, fruit juice, or milk. No cookies, donuts, pop, or sugary Koolaid this time.

Optional Body Affirmation Events

1. Write a will bequeathing your best body part to a friend.
2. Think of a CB handle that refers in a positive way to one of your body parts.
3. Nominate your best body part to be cast in bronze.
4. Choose a Mr. or Ms. "leg, eyes, smile, hips, muscle," etc., and give that person a sash to wear that declares the honor. Give a title to every participant.
5. Give each other back rubs, foot rubs, hand rubs, face rubs.
6. Sculpture in clay or play dough a figure that represents how each person sees himself or herself. Then redo the sculpture to represent how God sees them. Offer these sculptures to God in the closing devotion by forming all the clay into one big mixture. Reshape that into a symbol representing God's love for everyone.

Stumbling Around in the Dark
(Light and Darkness in Life)

by Phyllis E. Castens

Objectives

To look at those times when we grope around in our lives in darkness, searching for the tiniest flicker of light

To celebrate the "Sonshine" that lights and brightens our way to God and to each other

To celebrate Jesus, the true Light of the world and in our life

Materials Needed

> Newsprint sheet
> Markers or pens
> Copies of Scripture study
> Bibles
> Small candle for each participant

Introduction to Topic

Each of us has times when we grope around in our lives in darkness, searching for ways to crack that darkness with even the tiniest flicker of light. Loneliness sets in and an overwhelming blindness brings even greater trepidation and despair. No one seems to bring hope—only more despair through gossip, lack of commitment, and failure to listen. Is there no one to help us? Is there no door leading out of this blackness?

Then suddenly! Dawn comes! The Sonshine brightens and lights our way to God and to each other. With that, we clasp each other's hands and celebrate the true Light, the Light of our world and of our life!

Where there is darkness, Lord, may we be the rays of the Son to touch the gloom of lonely lives.

Icebreakers (30 min.)

A. Draw an unlit candle on a newsprint sheet. Label the wick with a time in your life when you felt "unlit" or "snuffed out." With the wax, the body of the candle, name a talent or gift you have that is unused. Finally identify the candleholder with a person or thing that is a stabilizing force in your life.

B. Name times when you've felt like a

> bug light
> floodlight
> neon light
> fluorescent light
> penlight

Share your drawings and light statements in groups of five or six people. Make sure that each person has a chance to share or pass if he or she wishes. The person whose birthday is closest to the longest day of sunlight (June 21) starts.

Scripture Study (30 min.)

1 John 2:7-11 (in unison):

> "Beloved, I am writing you no new commandment, but an old commandment which you had from the beginning; the old commandment is the word which you have heard. Yet I am writing you a new commandment, which is true in him and in you, because the darkness is passing away and the true light is already shining. He who says he is in the light and hates his brother is in the darkness still. He who loves his brother abides in the light, and in it there is no cause for stumbling. But he who hates his brother is in the darkness and walks in the darkness, and does not know where he is going, because the

darkness has blinded his eyes." (RSV)

In small groups of five to six, have youth share their responses with the others. Have every person share his or her statement to A before moving on to B and so forth.

- A. After reading the Scripture passage, I feel that
    - I am in darkness!
    - I walk in the Light!
    - Dusk is closing in on me!
    - The sunrise is coming and dissipating the darkness!
- B. To me, someone who says he or she is in the Light, but is really still in the darkness, is someone who . . .
- C. I feel God wants me to shine the Light to such a person by . . .
- D. When I stumble in the darkness, God reaches out and brings me the Light by . . .
- E. Read John 1:4–5, then complete the following sentence: "The one way I want to keep the true Light shining in my life is . . ."

Worship (10–15 min.)

Have each person spend some quiet time with his or her Bible. Find a passage that has particular meaning to you tonight. (Write it down on paper or mark the place in your Bible.)

Give each person a small candle. Have youth sit in a circle on the floor and turn out the lights. Have one person light his or her candle and share the Scripture chosen earlier and its meaning for his or her life with the person on his or her right. That person then lights his or her own candle and shares with the next person and so forth around the circle until all the candles are lit. Then join in the following responsive reading.

Responsive Reading

L: Lord, in my times of loneliness and despair,
R: let me feel You touching my life.
L: When I fail to give of myself to a friend,
R: give Your Son to be a friend and bring us back into the Light of friendship.
L: If rumors and gossip hurt me,
R: let me know that You are there with a shoulder to cry on and a hug to reassure me.
L: Lord, bring me to see that You are a personal God;
R: that You search for me wherever I am in the darkness of failure;
L: that You love me with Your amazing grace through Your Son, Jesus Christ.
R: Bring me into the Light, Jesus Christ, so that I may stand fully revealed, yet not ashamed.
All: Help me also to bring others to the Light, to know the warmth of the Son after the coldness and dampness of the dark. Amen.

Song

Sing "Walking in the Light" or "I am the Light of the World."

Recreation (30 min.)

Sardines

This game is similar to Hide 'n' Seek except that the person who's "it" hides, and the rest of the group searches for him or her. When a person finds "it's" hiding place, the person joins "it." The group continues to gather in the one place until the last person discovers the hiding place. The game can continue until the group tires of it, or until It runs out of hiding places.

Hint for more fun: Turn the lights out and choose small places—pack 'em in! (One restriction to enforce is that no one hides in the nave of the church or in the offices.)

Afterglow (15 min.)

Light refreshments, such as popcorn and apple cider, can be made available. Encourage ping pong, bumper-pool, or other nondirected fellowship.

Talking in the Light
(An Advent Night)

by Nancy Schmidt

Objective

To enable participants to reflect on the "Word made flesh" by taking a look at God's Word, and at our own words

Materials Needed

    Markers
    Sheets of newsprint
    Bibles
    Paper

Introduction to Topic

Advent is a special season in the church year, for it gives us an opportunity to anticipate and to prepare ourselves as we look to the coming of the Word in human form. Through this youth night we seek to enable participants to reflect upon the "Word made flesh" by taking a look at God's Word and at our own words.

Icebreaker (20-30 min.)

Before people arrive, you'll need to gather markers and a roll or sheet of newsprint. (Any of the larger newspapers or printers in your town have end rolls of newsprint that they throw away.) As people arrive, instruct each to tear off a large sheet of newsprint, and cut or tear a large hole in the center. This will create a poncho or "WONDERFUL WORD WEAR." Ask each person to decorate the front of his or her "WORD WEAR" with his or her favorite expression, and the back with ONE word that expresses something he or she is looking forward to this Advent. When all the youth have finished decorating, have them put their WONDERFUL WORD WEAR on. Instruct the group to play dictionary and look up all the different words and expressions exhibited in the WORD WEAR. If your group is well acquainted, you can switch WORD WEAR and try to guess who's from all those favorite expressions.

Learning Experience

Divide the group into smaller groups of five or six by numbering off or by having each person gather with four or five others exhibiting expressions that he or she *never* says.

Tell participants: During Advent we often hear words that we don't especially hear at any other time of the church year. Some of them are listed here. Choose your favorite Advent word and share it with your group. Tell them what it means to you.

Emmanuel	Advent	Prince of Peace
Waiting	Fulfillment	Preparation
Hope	(One of your own)	

Now read John 1:1-14. Choose one person in your group to read it out loud. Verse 4 refers to Jesus as the Source of light to humankind. Tell your group about one way that Jesus' coming *this*

Christmas will bring new light to your life . . .

The "Word," which comes from the Greek word "logos," means more than just speech. Here, the Word is God Himself in action . . . creating, redeeming, and revealing Himself to us. With that in mind, discuss and make a list of what differences you see in John 1 between God's Word and our words.

Verse 14 says that God's Word became flesh, a person, and lived with us. It is talking about God becoming incarnate in the Person of His Son Jesus. Scripture also affirms that God is active in people to carry out His purposes. To celebrate that, play the Match Game; it's a word association game.

Pass out pieces of paper to all the members of your group. Appoint one person as the "model" and have the remaining members of the group think of one positive word that describes that person. Have participants, in turn, hold up their cards and explain to that person why they think of him or her as "smiling" or "caring" or . . . . Then move on to the next person and repeat the process.

Worship

You'll want to choose a place to worship. You might want to go to another room to convey that worship is different and a special activity.

Begin singing "Walkin' in the Light." You could vary the choruses by inserting a new word each time, for example, Talkin' or Waitin' or Workin' or Playin'.

Invocation

- **L:** We interrupt our busy Christmas preparations to join together and await a Word from our God. It's a Word that brings light to the darkness of our days and hope to our hopeless world. It's a Word that is a name . . . and given in the name of the Father, and of the Son, and of the Holy Spirit. It's a Word that is a person, Jesus Christ, God with us.
- **A:** O Lord, I really have a small vocabulary. I try very hard, God, but I can't seem to learn any really *new* words by myself. Even while I am waiting to celebrate Jesus' birth, I still use the same old words with the people around me—words like "me first," "I'm lonely," "I hate," "I'm no good," "I won't," "I can't win," "give me," "I'm in darkness," "I'm alone," "I'm a sinner."
- **L:** I have a Word from God for you. That Word is Jesus Christ. Because God's Word is action, Jesus comes as God with us. He brings *new* words into our vocabulary. Words like "life," "resurrection," and "forgiveness." His birth is a Word from God that says, "I love you," and "You are mine." Jesus teaches us brand-new words to say to each other, too. "Because Jesus first loved me, I love you too." Try saying that to all the people around you. (*Begin to do that.*)

Song

Sing, "And God said, 'Yes.' "

Prayers

Remembering God's one Word, Jesus, try one-word prayers. They're just like chain prayers, except prayers are expressed in one word rather than in a sentence.

Blessing

Then gather together and close with one-word blessings. Ask each participant to think of a word that expresses a hope or a wish that he or she has for the other members of the group this Advent or Christmas season. Share them, and talk about them.

Afterglow

You can continue this play on words with some word games or refreshments. I'd suggest some appropriate "word" refreshments, such as Alpha Bits or Alphabet soup, but I don't think anyone would eat them!

So how about a dictionary game? You'll need to have a dictionary, paper, and pencils. Someone looks in the dictionary for an unusual word, announces it to the rest, and writes down the definition. Everyone else makes up his or her own definition. The definitions are shuffled, and each player grabs one to read aloud to the group. The game is guessing which is the correct definition and which are fakes!

Or play Prui and learn a new word. You see, a Prui is actually a very warm, snuggly thing of which everyone wants to be a part. The game goes like this: Each player is blindfolded or closes his or her eyes. The leader designates one person as the Prui, who is not allowed to talk. All the other players will walk around and search for the Prui. When they come upon another person, the players ask, "Prui?" If the person responds, "Prui"; it's not the Prui. (Pruis don't talk). But if the person does NOT answer, AH HA! It's the Prui! The player then joins hands with the Prui (but only at the end of the line if there is more than one person in the Prui). As a part of the Prui, the players need to remember not to talk either. The game ends when everyone is part of the warm, snuggly Prui!

This game is an oldie but a goodie. The group sits in a circle. The leader begins with a prop, such as a spoon. He or she hands it to the person on the right and says, "This is a spoon." The person must then respond by saying, "a what?" The leader answers, "a spoon." The person then hands it on with, "This is a spoon." "A what?" "A what?" (All questions must go back to the leader.) The leader can then begin an object in the other direction, adding to the fun and confusion!

In Whose Image?
(An Epiphany Night)

by Margaret Rickers

Objectives

To help youth see themselves as "images" or "reflections" of their parents, friends, and God
To help youth see themselves as God's "lights" in the lives of other people
To help youth realize that we all see each other in a different "light"

Material Needed

Supply of old magazines
Different sizes and colors of paper
Scissors
Glue
Marking pens
Bibles
Learning experience sheets

Get-Acquainted Activity

As the youth arrive, direct them to an area you have prepared ahead of time. The area (preferably covered tables) should be equipped with a supply of old magazines, different sizes and colors of paper, scissors, glue, and different colored marking pens.

Youth should create three "pictures" of themselves out of the materials provided. The "pictures" should depict (a) how I see myself, (b) how my parents see me, and (c) how my friends see me.

Give the youth about 20 to 25 minutes to create their own "pictures" of themselves. Point out that these could be a drawing, a collage, a symbol, or a three-dimensional creation. After everyone has had adequate time to create his or her "pictures," gather the whole group together in a circle.

Have each youth share one or more of the pictures as he or she feels comfortable doing, particularly pointing out why he or she thinks he or she is seen that way. Display the creations in the youth room or on a bulletin board for the remainder of the evening or longer, if feasible.

Learning Experience

(Sufficient copies of the Bible study material that begins with item 3 should be made for all youth.)

1. Divide the group into small clusters of six to eight people. The leader of each cluster is the person whose first name is closest to the letter I in the alphabet (if there are two or more people who qualify, use the last names too). Encourage group members to get to know each other better. Have them move around the circle and "shed some light" on themselves by sharing a characteristic they have that is like a parent, a brother or sister, or a friend. (These can be physical traits, habits, words they use, etc.)
2. Luther suggests to us that we be "little Christs" to one another. We can all probably identify some significant individual in our lives who has made an impact on us—maybe even someone who has been a "little Christ" to us or who has been a bright and positive light in our past. Have youth identify that person—first name only—and share with the group why that person has been significant to them.
3. Read Gen. 1:26–27 as a small group. List things that would have been different if we had remained in the "image and perfection of God" like Adam and Eve before the fall into sin. Have a "light-hearted" conversation about it—dream and imagine with your group.
4. Check out 1 Cor. 12 as a group. Name different gifts that are suggested by this passage. What gifts would help you fit the image you would like to have or help you be a "light" to someone else? What gifts do you see in others that are reflections of Christ? Share with the group.
5. Two options below can be decided on either by the group or by the youth counselor.

    ### Option 1: Image Contracts

    Give each group member an index card. Have each person write the words "Image Contract" across the top. Ask each youth to spend a few minutes alone thinking about his or her own image and ways to improve part of it. Have youths write a sentence or two in "self-contracts" about ways this could be accomplished. For example, one contract might read: "I will make every effort to be more pleasant and cooperative around home in order to improve my image with my family."

    ### Option 2: You Light Up My Life

    The youth should reflect on someone who stands out as an especially bright light in their minds—someone whom they would like to thank for being a positive image for them. The youth counselor should prepare cards ahead of time by duplicating or photocopying index cards or paper with these words: When we talked about positive "lights" and "images" in our lives in a Bible study today, I thought of you because for me you have been _____. I thank God for your sharing your light with me.

    The youth fills in the person's name whom they see as the "image" or "light" as well as the reason they feel this way (for example, "a friend when I was down" or "a listening ear when I needed you"). The youth should sign their cards and, if they choose, address and mail them or give them to the people in person.

6. Close this Bible study with a circle or "popcorn" prayer. Sing an appropriate hymn, such as "Father, We Bless Thee."

Recreation

Recreation activities depend on your geographical location. If you are in the "snow belt," make snow sculptures. (Be sure to warn the youth in advance so they can come with appropriate outdoor gear.) Create "images" in the snow by having a snow sculpture contest.

You could also play some indoor mirroring games. Have each youth find a partner. One of the pair decides on a series of actions that he or she will do while the other person stands in front of him or her, facing front-to-front and imitating the actions as if he or she were looking in a mirror. (In other words, the actions will be opposite.) No doubt this activity will end up with everyone rolling on the floor with laughter!

Afterglow

Refreshments could be simple snacks or a fun baking activity that carries through the theme of "images." Prepare an easy sugar cookie recipe and gather as many different cookie cutters as possible. (Ask the youth to bring some from home, too.) The youth will have a great time rolling out the dough, cutting different "images" cookies, and decorating them with frosting or colored sugars. The cookies only take a few minutes to bake, so the youth will be able to devour their refreshments quickly after the cutting and decorating.

Suggestion: Encourage the youth to share their cookies with residents of a nearby nursing home or home for handicapped people. These people will love being remembered at times other than Christmas. It will help to light up their lives!

Growing Through Grieving

by Miriam Conradi-Meyer

Objectives

To enable participants to handle effectively personal grief in coping with death, impending death, divorce, or major loss
To help participants identify the five stages of grieving
To help participants to celebrate the company of fellow Christian young people

Materials Needed

    Construction paper
    Magazines
    Glue
    Scissors
    Markers
    Situation papers
    Bibles

Get in Gear (30 min.)

Give youth the following instructions:

1. Make a name tag, choosing a color that fits the mood you are presently experiencing.
2. Above your name, draw or glue a magazine picture of something you have lost or misplaced in the past.
3. Below your name, draw or paste a picture of something you now have that you would hate to lose.
4. Somewhere else on the tag, name a friend or family member who moved away or died.
5. Get in a group of five people. Quickly go around the circle and share the information on your name tags, explaining each of the four items.

Grow and Learn (30 min.)

Elisabeth Kubler-Ross, M.D., after years of experience with sick, old, and dying patients, produced an excellent resource on the stages of grieving for coping with death and dying. It's been found that we usually go through these stages in response to any loss in our lives. The following adaptation is developed from the exciting findings she and numerous others that support these concepts have made.

A. Write the following on bulletin board, chalkboard, or newsprint:

Five Stages of Grieving

Stage 1: Denial—Temporary state of shock and disbelief. "No, it can't be true!" "There must be some mistake."
Stage 2: Anger—Rage, envy, resentment at self, others, or God. "Why me?" "It's not fair." "If only I'd . . ."
Stage 3: Bargaining—Making a deal or promise. "If I'm real good and don't do that, everything will be okay."
Stage 4: Depression—Sense of great loss, deep hurt, and frustration. "I don't feel like doing anything anymore."
Stage 5: Acceptance—Rest, quiet peace, more hopeful feeling. "It hurts, but I'm going to be okay now."

B. Have youth divide into teams, approximately five people on each team.
C. Distribute to each team five slips of paper on which have been written the five questions that follow the description of Situation 1 below. Read the description of the situation, then have each team label the quotations on the slips of paper they have received according to the five stages of grieving and put them in order. The team that does this correctly the fastest is the winner. Repeat the process with Situations 2 and 3.

Situation 1

Death: Ron is called from his classroom by the principal. He is told that his mother has just been killed in a car accident.

Key

Stage 1 "It's really somebody else. It can't be true. Maybe she's just hurt real bad."
Stage 5 "It sure hurts. I miss my mom a lot, but I guess I'll make it."
Stage 3 "Please don't let it be. I promise I'll go to Bible class and church, if you only make it all be just a bad dream."
Stage 4 "The house is so empty without her. I don't feel like cleaning my room or seeing friends."
Stage 2 "Why did God let this happen? He doesn't care. He probably doesn't even exist!"

Situation 2

Divorce: Jan's parents have just left for the lawyer's office. They're talking about getting a divorce.

Key

Stage 4 "Who cares. Nothing works out for me anymore. What's the use?"
Stage 3 "Maybe if I fix supper for them and stay home tonight, they'll be in a better mood and work everything out."
Stage 1 "They're not really going to get a divorce. They can't. This hassle will blow over like the rest."
Stage 5 "Lots of people get divorces. I guess God will help me through this, too. I'm not alone."
Stage 2 "Stupid Dad. If he wasn't so stubborn and bullheaded, . . ."

Situation 3

Loss: Guy tried out for the basketball team. The roster has been posted on the locker room bulletin board. His name is not on it.

Key

Stage 5 "Looks like I'm not going to be playing on the basketball team this year like I'd hoped, but I do like to sing. Maybe I'll try the school choir for a change."
Stage 2 "Stupid coach! What does he know anyway? He always plays favorites."
Stage 1 "There's been a mistake! They forgot to type my name on the list!"
Stage 3 "If I help a lot during physical education class, maybe I'll take somebody's

place when they get sick or move away."

Stage 4 "I did not make the basketball team. I'm really disappointed. I feel so left out when my friends go to practice."

Keep in mind that the length of time that a person takes to experience each stage in a crisis will vary. It may take a few minutes or a few years to resolve the feelings.

Also, these are natural stages that we go through. It is healthy to experience the stages and not block or stifle their expression.

These stages could also be applied to breaking up with a boyfriend or girlfriend, moving away from friends, or other traumatic events.

Option

Try to think up your own examples for each stage. Imagine a shocking situation and have the teams race to see which can come up with appropriate quotes for each stage.

Bible Study

Read together Ps. 23. In small groups, have each person verbally share the following sentence completions:

1. A time that I have felt as if I were "walking through the valley of the shadow of death" was when . . .
2. In Matt. 28:20, Christ says, "Lo, I am with you always, to the end of the age" (RSV). When I hear that, I think . . .
3. Read 2 Cor. 4:7–12. "We are afflicted . . . but not crushed . . ." (v.8) tells me . . .

Glorifying and Giving Thanks (10–15 min.)

Sing the song: "For Those Tears I Died" (Come to the Water) by Marsha J. Stevens.

V: Lord, we praise and adore You,
R: for You are all-knowing and seeing.
V: A sparrow does not fall to the ground
R: without your knowledge.
V: When I am in pain and suffering because of my sins,
R: You are a forgiving God.
V: I become angry at You and deny You;
R: I blame others for my hurt.
V: I try to work it out myself;
R: I don't trust You.
V: Thank You, that through the blood of Christ
All: we are forgiven, redeemed, strengthened, and set free.
V: Lord, we praise and adore You,
R: for You give us hope.
V: Sometimes I get frustrated, hurt, and discouraged.
R: Sometimes I feel crushed, lethargic, and depressed.
V: But You are always by my side.
R: You give me strength and courage.
V: You give me peace and rest.
All: You give me the hope and joy of eternal life.

Song: "A Mighty Fortress"

Goodies to Gobble and Good Fun, Too! (45 min.)

An enjoyable refreshment and fellowship treat is to make pizza together. There are usually jobs for everyone, such as slicing mushrooms, chopping onion, grating cheese, cooking hamburger, cutting sausage, mixing dough, spreading tomato sauce, etc. Each youth could draw a card with his/her task listed.

This activity provides yummy results also. While the oven is busily baking the delicious-smelling pizzas, a game of Frisbee football or Nerf ball keep-away could be played.

Life Is Forgiving

by George Guidera

Objectives

To help youth better understand why breaking up is painful
To help youth better cope with those times when someone breaks a relationship with them
To help youth gain insight into how to help others when they experience broken relationships in their lives
To help free youth to continue loving others after having experienced a broken relationship

Materials Needed

3" x 5" cards
Pencils
Bibles
"Dear Abner" letters
Newsprint

Introduction to Topic

Almost everyone experiences at least one broken relationship at sometime in his or her life. While that may be true, it is not a very helpful thing to say to a youth the day after his or her steady has returned a ring. The young person has to be helped to realize that the broken relationship does not mean the end of everything, and that it may even signal new beginnings.

But how can young people learn to accept the end of a relationship and continue to risk loving others? And how can they help one another to work through the pain of broken relationships?

Perhaps the basic problem many young people have when a relationship is broken occurs because they have not really understood why we enter into relationships. Too many times, perhaps, youth enter into relationships solely for their own benefit rather than for the mutual benefit of both parties involved in the relationship (for example, going steady with the prettiest cheerleader or the best athlete in the school because it makes the young person an important person in the eyes of his or her peers, instead of going steady because the two individuals enjoy many of the same activities and find real joy in sharing these).

A healthy relationship involves "give and take." But when one enters into a relationship for purely selfish reasons, it is all "take" and no "give." When a breakup occurs in such a relationship, the one who entered into the relationship for selfish reasons sees the breakup in terms of something he or she has had taken away.

To understand God's giving and forgiving love is to learn how to give to another as an essential part of one's relationship with that person. And to understand the concept that giving is an important aspect of any relationship will help youth to better deal with the pain of a broken relationship. For when a relationship includes giving as an essential ingredient, one can accept the break much more easily and forgive the hurt. For one's primary concern will not be with his or her loss, but with the happiness and well-being of the other person. Knowing and understanding this will help youth better cope with those times when they face broken relationships and will give them insight into how to help others heal when they experience broken relationships in their lives.

Icebreaker (30 min.)

Distribute to each person a 3" x 5" index card. On one side of the card, ask each person to complete this statement:

"My best male friend is _____

because he _____."

On the other side of the card, ask each person to complete this statement:

"My best female friend is _____

because she _____."

Ask each person to choose a partner (not one of the persons identified on his or her card). Partners are to tell each other who they identified on their cards and the reasons they consider these people their best friends.

After about 10 minutes, reassemble the group. On the chalkboard or on a large sheet of newsprint, write two-column headings: "Reasons for Friendship with Someone of the Same Sex" and "Reasons for Friendship with Someone of the Opposite Sex." Divide the space under these headings into two columns: "Reasons That Benefit Me" and "Reasons That Benefit the Other Person."

Ask youth to volunteer the reasons for their friendships which they wrote on their cards. (They need not reveal the names they wrote.) Have the group decide—perhaps by voting—into which category each reason for friendship falls, then write that reason in the appropriate column. Note that the reasons for some friendships—probably the most ideal ones—may fall into both categories.

Note: Some reasons youth give for their friendships may be humorous, and some may be given in an attempt to shock the group. Be ready to deal with these without being harsh or judgmental. Record them in the appropriate column even though the responses may seem inappropriate. You may discover that the humor or the attempt to shock masks some deep thoughts or feelings.

Bible Study (40 min.)

1. Ask the group to turn to 1 John 4:7–11. Have someone read this passage out loud, then discuss the following questions:

   a. What is the nature of God's relationship with us?
   b. What example does God's relationship with us give us to follow in our relationship with others?
   c. What is the basis for our relationships—even our romantic relationships—with others?
   d. How will this show itself in our interaction with those with whom we are in relationships?
   e. How will understanding this help when a steady or a friend breaks a relationship?
   f. How will understanding this help me to provide healing for another when he or she experiences a broken relationship?

2. Ask the group to turn to 1 Cor. 13:4–7 and read this passage aloud. If you accept the premise that all relationships have their source in God's relationship with us, then this passage, although it deals first of all with God's love for us, can also be applied to our love for others—including the love that expresses itself in romantic or friendship relationships. Have the group discuss the following questions:

   a. What does this passage have to say about the nature of our relationships with others?
   b. How will what this passage says about love show itself in our interaction with those with whom we are in relationship?
   c. How will this understanding of love help me provide healing for another when he or she experiences a broken relationship?

3. Now youth will have an opportunity to apply what they have learned in their study of the two Bible passages above. They will do this by trying their hand at giving "advice to the lovelorn."

   Divide participants into three groups. Give each group a copy of one of the three "Dear Abner" letters printed below. Ask members of each group to read and discuss the letter they have been given, then write a response to that letter.

   Bring the groups back together and have a spokesperson for each group read the group's response. If time permits, allow members of the other groups to comment on the group's response and offer further suggestions about how the letter might have been answered.

Group 1

Dear Abner,

    I have a real problem. I'm ugly! I have waited for years to be asked out. Finally a guy asked me out, but all he wants to do is park. Last night he told me we were finished because I wouldn't go far enough with him. Abner, I really want to have a boyfriend, but I've been taught all my life that some things are wrong. I've been crying all day over what to do. What should I do?

                                                                                                                     Lonesome

Group 2

Dear Abner,

    Sue and I have been going together for over a year. All of a sudden she wants to go out with other guys besides me. She still wants us to be friends and to go out, but she also wants the freedom to go out with others. I don't want her to go out with other guys. We make a nice couple, and she is lots of fun to be with. We have a lot of things in common, and everybody says we are great together. What can I say to her?

                                                                                                                      Confused

Group 3

Dear Abner,

    There is this real dreamy guy at school. He plays on the basketball team, has a super car, and is a great dancer. All the girls go crazy over him. We've gone out several times and had a great time, but he also goes out with other girls. About two weeks ago I hinted strongly to him that I wanted to be his steady, and since that time he's hardly spoken to me and hasn't asked me out again. What should I do?

                                                                                                    Frustrated

Worship (15 min.)

    Sing, "They'll Know We Are Christians by Our Love" or another song that deals with our oneness in Christ.

    Comment on the fact that the Lord provides help and hope for us when we experience broken relationships, even at those times when we have broken our relationship with Him. To emphasize this, read or have someone else read Lam. 3:1–9, 19–33.

    Ask youth to offer a prayer for God's strength for those who are suffering the pain of broken relationships.

Recreation (15 min.)

    "Darling, if you love me, won't you please smile?" would be a good game to play.

    Begin with the group sitting in a circle. Choose someone to be It. It goes to someone of the opposite sex and asks, "Darling, if you love me, won't you please smile?" The person asked must respond, "Darling, you know I love you, but I just can't smile." He or she must say this without smiling.

    It may ask the same person the question up to three times. If the person responding smiles while answering, that person becomes It. If the person responding does not smile, It moves on to another person and asks that person the question. By the way, you can't close your eyes when responding, and tickling is forbidden.

Refreshment (20 min.)

    Let youth experience the "give and take" of a relationship by having them divide into pairs and having the pairs make fresh-fruit ice-cream sundaes for each other. Determine the pairings by drawing names. Provide lemonade or a hot drink to accompany the sundaes. This should provide a good ending to an evening of activities focusing on relationships!

The Feelings of Others
(Communicating Feelings)

by Susan K. Wendorf

Objectives

To help youth focus on how they respond to the feelings of others
To help youth identify and express their feelings
To help youth accept the feelings of others

Materials Needed

    Old magazines
    Pins
    Newsprint
    Bibles
    15 4" x 12" pieces of posterboard

Introduction to Topic: Responding to Other's Feelings

This Youth Night moves the focus from recognizing and accepting my feelings to beginning to respond to and accept others' feelings. It is a logical progression. If we can accept the fact that we have feelings of guilt, loneliness, anger, and abandonment—as well as feelings of joy, satisfaction, accomplishment, peace, and togetherness—then it is easier for us to identify, accept, and respond to those feelings in others.

With this in mind, and with what we have learned from "Believe Me," we can begin tonight to deal with the feelings of others. Responding to others' feelings means, first, that we help them to identify their feelings, and secondly, to *express* their feelings. Once they have identified and expressed their feelings, it is our turn to *accept* the feelings they have shared with us.

Icebreaker/Get-Acquainted Activity

This activity, which should be about half an hour long, is designed to serve a twofold purpose: it will help people become acquainted and introduce the evening's theme in a low-key manner.

Gather a variety of pictures from old magazines. They can be pictures of plants, animals, outdoor scenes, city scenes—anything *except* people. Have enough so that each person gets one picture. As the young people arrive, pin a picture on their sleeves (or, if they're sleeveless, as close to the shoulder as possible). They should be able to see their own picture and it should be visible to everyone else.

Instruct each person to decide what feeling or emotion his or her picture represents. Tell the youth to choose one word that describes that feeling but not to say that word aloud to anyone else. Then instruct them to find one or more persons with a picture that they think expresses the same emotion as their own picture. All of this should be done nonverbally. When everyone has found at least one "match" (there might be as many as five or six in a group), let the youth begin talking to find out if they do, in fact, match. Some groups may have to find new partners—for example, one person might have chosen the word "quiet" to describe her picture's feelings, only to find out that her "match" chose "lonely" to describe his picture. There will probably be some negotiating going on as people try to convince each other that their pictures express the same feelings. That's okay.

Remember that this is just an icebreaker—a way to open communication among the youth and perhaps to introduce them to the idea that similar situations can elicit different feelings.

Allow about 30 minutes for the activity. The process need not be "finished" when the allotted time is gone, or it may take less time. If you have a small group, for instance, and everyone is satisfied that good picture-feeling matches have been made after only 10 minutes, that's fine. Continue the process by bringing the whole group together to "judge" whether good matches were made between pictures and feelings.

Learning Experience

Read Mark 4:35-41, "Jesus Calms the Storm," and discuss the reading in small groups for seven to eight minutes. Here are questions to lead the discussion:

    What were the feelings of the disciples?
    What were Jesus' feelings?
    How did the disciples respond to Jesus' tiredness?
    Why did they respond as they did?
    How did Jesus respond to the feelings of the disciples?

Read Mark 14:32-34, "Jesus in Gethsemane." Again, discuss the reading in small groups, but this time allow only five to six minutes. Questions:

    What were Jesus' feelings?
    What were the feelings of the disciples?
    How did Jesus respond to the disciples' tiredness?
    Why did He respond that way?
    How did the disciples respond to the feelings of Jesus?

After talking about the feelings that are stated or implied in these two incidents between Jesus and the disciples, take 15 or 20 minutes to have groups roleplay the scenes. Follow the Scripture accounts as closely as possible.

Encourage the cast to "get into" their characters—to express the anger, the fear, the disappointment, the exhaustion. If the group is large enough, and if time permits, you may want to repeat the roleplays to involve as many youth as possible.

With the whole group, discuss the readings and the roleplaying. Was it difficult to roleplay a Jesus with emotion? Did the youth find it equally difficult to roleplay the disciples? What might explain the differences/similarities in the roles? Is it okay to be angry . . . disappointed . . . frustrated . . . impatient? When . . . why . . . how? What are some good ways to respond to someone else's anger . . . disappointment . . . impatience? What have you learned from these Scripture passages about responding to the feelings of others? What might have happened if Jesus had not responded to the disciples' fear in the boat? Think of a time when someone did not respond to your fear—and of a time when you did not respond to someone else's fear. Why do people sometimes show a different emotion than the one they are really feeling? If we suspect that is happening, should we respond to the feeling that's showing or to the one that's not showing? Why?

Worship

Beforehand prepare 15 4" x 12" blank pieces of posterboard. Gather the group into a circle. Have the group think of 25 different feelings. As they call out the feelings, write one on each piece of posterboard. Place an offering basket in the center of the circle and distribute the completed feeling cards among the group.

Begin with the prayer, "Lord, teach us to accept and respond to these feelings in others . . . ." Ask the people with the feeling cards to say the feeling aloud as they place the cards in the basket, one at a time. Close with one or two of the group's favorite songs or hymns. Let the youth decide what they feel like singing. (Be ready with one or two song ideas—perhaps the offertory from the liturgy—in case no one suggests a song.)

If you have a youth room, you may want to suggest the group post the feeling cards up on the walls after worship.

Recreation

Invite one of the youths to play the role of a check-out person. You assume the other role. Introduce the skit in your own words or say, "This story really happened. The scene is a large supermarket in a medium-sized midwestern city. It is a busy Saturday afternoon in October. ME has a cart full of groceries and has just begun to unload at the check-out. SHE is a supermarket checker and has just begun to ring up the prices. ME and SHE are strangers to one another. As always, Muzak is playing "buy it" music on the store's loudspeaker system."

She (barely glancing up): Hi, how are you?
Me: Fine, thanks, and you?
She: Fine.
Me: Why?
She (still ringing up groceries): I beg your pardon?
Me: Why?
She: Why what?
Me: Why are you fine?
She: Oh. Why am I fine? *(She smiles slightly.)* Well, actually I'm not fine, if you really want to know.
Me (still unloading groceries): Sure.
She: Well, I've been working for six hours, and my feet are really tired. *(She stops ringing up groceries.)* Everyone's in a rush. We've been so busy today that I didn't get a break this afternoon, and besides that, I've got a sinus headache.
Me: And I bet you'd rather be outside.
She: Yeah. Is it as nice outside as it looks?
Me: It's beautiful. *(She moans.)* But I heard on the radio we're supposed to have a hard frost tonight. That should help your sinuses, shouldn't it?
She: I guess so. *(She resumes ringing up groceries upon noticing the growing line of impatient customers.)*
Me: Have you taken anything for your headache?
She: Yeah, but it didn't help.
Me: I'm no expert, but when one of those hits me, I sometimes take *(name brand)*. Have you ever tried it?
She: No. Maybe, I will.
Me: It usually works for me.
She (handing Me the change): Well, there you are. Hey, it was nice meeting you.
Me: Thanks. It was nice meeting you too. Hope the rest of your day goes better.
She (laughing): Oh, it will. I'm off in 45 minutes, and I'm going to a party tonight. Bye.
Me: Bye. Take care.

At the conclusion of the skit add: "Breaking through the hi-how-are-you-fine-how-are-you with a 'why' doesn't always turn out to be such a neat experience. But it's a start toward helping others identify and express their feelings and then responding to them.

"For recreation tonight we are going to visit our local shopping center (or cluster of stores). Scatter out in twos or threes to different stores. Make an inexpensive purchase, such as a pack of gum, an ice-cream cone, or a box of tissues. When you check out, try adding a "why" to the hi-how-are-you-fine-how-are-you exchange with the cashier. In 10 or 15 minutes we will regroup in the parking lot. When we come back, we will share our experiences."

Afterglow

For refreshments, encourage the youth to deal in a practical manner with other's feelings by providing a variety of refreshments (for example, two apples, three brownies, one hamburger, a couple of small bags of munchies, some carrot sticks, a peanut butter and jelly sandwich, an orange, a small carton of milk, three cans of pop, etc.) so that the youth have to choose one refreshment, depending on what each feels like eating. Sharing, bartering, exchanging, negotiating—all these—can become a part of the afterglow. Be sure everyone gets something to eat and that it stays on the fun side of the learning experience.

Give It All You've Got
(Money and Our Giving)

by Paula Mott Becker

Objectives

To build awareness of priorities for spending money

To understand giving better as an opportunity to enrich and strengthen our relationship to God and others

Materials Needed

    Posterboard
    Construction paper
    Beans
    Pens
    Box

Icebreaker: The Story of Life Game

Preparation

Prior to the evening, the leader will need to do the following:

1. Write the name of each "store" (see sample) on a piece of posterboard and list the items and "costs." (You may add or subtract items according to needs of your group.)
2. Cut construction paper cards (approximately 2 1/2" by 4 1/2"). You'll need seven different colors for each different "store." The number of cards will depend on the size of the group. (The sample has the approximate number for 15 participants.)
3. Gather a supply of beans, buttons, etc., to serve as "money."
4. Hang the posters or place them on tables around the room. Beneath each "store," place the appropriate color cards, several pens, and a box.
5. If desired, place a sign on the door that says "The Store of Life."

Playing the Game

As participants arrive, have them browse through the "stores" to get an idea of what is available. After everyone has arrived, explain the following rules:

1. People with brown eyes receive 50 beans.
2. People with blue or green eyes must do 5 sit-ups, 15 jumping jacks, and then another 5 sit-ups and 10 jumping jacks for 25 beans. (Those who choose to do nothing may try to borrow beans from those who have them.)
3. Players may buy any item from a "store" and spend (or save) all their beans, plus whatever they can borrow from others.
4. The player must place the indicated number of beans in the box next to the store where the item is purchased.

Allow 15 to 20 minutes for "shopping."

Reflection (20 min.)

After all transactions have been made, ask the group to divide into groups of six. (Make sure there are both brown-eyed and blue-eyed people in each group.) Discuss:

1. Blue-eyed people: How did you feel about having to work for the beans you got? Did it make a difference in how you spent them?
2. Brown-eyed people: How did you feel about receiving free beans while others had to work?
3. If you borrowed beans, what did you buy with them?
4. Put your cards in order of importance to you. Is this the order in which you bought them? Why or why not?
5. At what store did you spend most of your beans? Are these the items on which you spend

    most of your money in daily life?
  6. How did you decide what to buy and what not to buy?
  7. How many of your beans were spent on yourself? Others? Savings?
  8. At the store what was the greatest number of beans spent by your group? The second greatest? Does this say anything about our needs or priorities? Why or why not?

Bible Study (20 min.)

Ask the group to come together and briefly share some comments about their findings from reflection time. How many of the total group spent some of their beans for donations, offerings, or gifts?

Complete these sentences and write down your thoughts:
  1. People give because
  2. Real giving means
  3. Giving shows

Read together the story of the widow's mite in Mark 12:41–44. Discuss:
  1. If you had been there, how would you feel about what the widow did?
  2. What words do you think describe the widow's relationship with God?
  3. Name some excuses she could have used for not giving her mite?
  4. What do you think the widow's gift meant to her?
  5. Identify some characteristics of a giving person.
  6. What excuses do we use for not giving?
  7. What does the story of the widow teach us about sacrifices in giving? About the responsibility to God in giving? About the privilege of giving?

Worship (15 min.)

Finish this litany about ways we can give ourselves to God and to each other. Drawing from your discussion, add things that you can do as individuals or as a group. When your ideas are complete, speak the litany together with one person serving as reader.

All: Help us, Lord, to give of ourselves,
Reader: to listen to people when they hurt.
All: Help us, Lord, to give of ourselves,
Reader: to laugh with people when they are happy.
All: Help us, Lord, to give of ourselves,
Reader: to set aside some of our earnings to give back to You.
All: Help us, Lord, to give of ourselves,
Reader: to smile at someone and brighten his or her day.
All: Help us, Lord, to give of ourselves . . .

Close by singing, "Father, We Bless."

Recreation (45 min.)

Go on a scavenger hunt to collect canned goods or nonperishable food items to give to the needy. After the scavenger hunt enjoy refreshments and discuss the group or organization to which you want to donate the canned goods. Plan how best to present them.

The Store of Life

School Store	Beans	Transportation Store	Beans
Books	1	Gasoline	5
Supplies	3	Car insurance	3
Sports events	3	Motorcycle insurance	2
Cheerleading outfit	7	Bus fare	2
Sports uniform	7	Bicycle upkeep	2
Drill team uniform	7	Car maintenance	3
Dances	4	Motorcycle maintenance	2
Club fees (choir, band, etc.)	3		

Church Store	Beans
Special donations	2
Offering	4
Youth group dues	1
Parties	1
Retreats	5

Fun Store	
Movie	4
Rollerskating	2
Bowling	2
Vacations	5
Hayrides	3
Horseback riding	3
Eating out with friends	4
Dates	6
Plays	8
Waterslide	3
Music lessons	4
Dance lessons	4
Concerts	8
Skiing	6

Gift Store	Beans
Special occasions (graduation, confirmation, wedding)	3
Birthday	5
Anniversary	2
Christmas	8

Department Store	
Clothes	10
Junk food	2
Jewelry	3
Make-up	2
Books for enjoyment	4
Shaving needs	2
Records or tapes	5
Nylons	2
Games	5
Cigarettes	2
Shoes	6
Stationery	2
Purse	5
Stereo equipment	9
Rollerskates	8
Bowling ball	8
Skate board	7
Bicycle	15
Baseball bat	4
Baseball mitt	6
Football	6
Baseball	4
Tennis racket	7
Tennis balls	2
Ski equipment	13

Savings Store

Specify amount you wish to save and print the number on your card.___

Store	Color	Cards
School	Red	45
Transportation	Green	25
Church	Yellow	50
Fun	Blue	60
Gift	Orange	50
Department	Pink	80
Savings	Tan	15

A Time for Giving
(An Advent Night)

by Gregory Otte

Objectives

To be newly aware of our "gifting" God
To understand our response to God's gifts to us as worship
To see worship as praise and service to God and to God's people

Materials Needed

    Bibles
    Newsprint or large sheets of paper
    Markers
    Construction paper
    Scissors, hobby knife, or single-edged razor blade
    Pencils
    Colored pens or crayons
    Glue or paste

Icebreaker

Begin the evening by playing a game—a variation of Rock-Paper-Scissors. Divide the room into three zones: a free zone at each end and a playing zone in the middle. Divide the group into two teams. Tell members of both teams to huddle and decide which symbol they will "throw" with their hands: rock, paper, or scissors. The two teams form lines facing each other in the middle of the playing zone. All members chant, "Rock-Paper-Scissors," and both teams "throw" the chosen symbol. The winning symbol is determined as follows: rock breaks scissors, paper covers rock, scissors cut paper. (If both teams "throw" the same symbol, neither team wins, and the process is repeated.)

Members of the team with the winning symbol must tag the members of the losing team before they reach the free zone. A person who is tagged joins the winning/tagging team. The teams then huddle, decide on a symbol, and repeat the process described above.

After about 20 minutes, come together for a song. Some possibilities include "Come, O Jesus," "Gentle Mary Laid Her Child," and "O Come, O Come, Emmanuel."

Bible Study (30 min.)

Advent is a time when we think about gifts. We decide on, purchase, and wrap gifts for other people, and we wonder about and hope for gifts that we will receive. God is also very much in the "gift-giving business," especially at this time of year.

Consider the following Bible passages, identify the gift God is giving in each one, and write that gift on newsprint on the wall. (If the passage brings to mind other gifts of God, write those on the newsprint also.)

Gen. 2:7	John 10:28	Luke 4:10
1 Kings 3:5, 9	John 14:16	Luke 12:32
Ps. 106:1	John 14:27	John 4:14
Is. 7:14	John 15:16	John 6:27
Is. 56:5	John 16:23	John 17:2
Jer. 3:15	Matt. 7:11	Eph. 1:5-7
Jer. 24:7	Matt. 11:28	Eph. 1:17
Jer. 31:31	Matt. 16:19	Eph. 2:8
Matt. 6:11	Mark 10:45	Rev. 2:7
John 6:51	Luke 1:77, 79	Rev. 2:10

Add to this list some gifts of God that are meaningful to you, for example, joy, family, and friends.

Response (20–30 min.)

Our response to God's gifts is worship. Talk together, either in small groups or as one large group (seven is a good group number), about the following statements on worship:

1. Worship is a response to the gifts of God. When we recognize and appreciate God's gifts, then our worship will be _____.
2. In and through our worship we recognize and acknowledge that God gives us everything we need graciously, freely, and liberally. This will move us to _____.
3. Worship does not only happen in formal gatherings. It occurs throughout our daily lives. Some daily activities that are identifiable as worship are _____.
4. Christian worship is rooted in the Christian community. It flows from a participating group

of people. This means that Christian worship, in order to be most meaningful, should be
_____.
5. Christian service is intimately tied to Christian worship. Through worship we are inspired and enabled to put into practice the peace, joy, and love that God has given us in and through Jesus Christ. In our daily lives, this will mean that _____.
6. I feel most comfortable in a worship service when _____.
7. If I were the worship leader next Sunday, I would _____.

Sharing God's Gifts (30 min.)

Advent calendars have been used in the church for many years as a way to heighten expectation and hope for Christmas time, the time when God gave the greatest gift of all, His Son to be our Savior. In this activity, youth will work individually or in pairs to make Advent calendars that illustrate or identify some of God's gifts to us.

Make the Advent calendars as follows:
1. Using pencils or felt-tip pens, draw a 1/4-inch border around two 10" x 14" sheets of construction paper.
2. Divide the space inside the border on each sheet into 26 rectangular spaces of equal size.
3. On one sheet of construction paper, draw a line through each of the 26 rectangles to divide them in half lengthwise.
4. Using a scissors, hobby knife, or sharp, single-edged razor blade, cut along the line dividing the rectangles and on a line just above and just below the top and bottom lines of each rectangle to form "windows."
5. Beginning with November 30 (St. Andrew's Day) and ending with Christmas Day, December 25, write the date on each window. (St. Andrew's Day is a good day with which to begin an Advent calendar. It is the start of the new church year, and Andrew was given the gift of being the first disciple called by Jesus, a gift he shared by bringing others to Jesus. See John 1:40–41 and John 6:8–9.)
6. Think about the gifts of God listed on the newsprint, gifts that may have been identified in the group discussions on worship, and other gifts of God. Draw a picture or symbol or write a Bible passage or other words in each of the 26 rectangles on the second sheet of construction paper.
7. Spread a thin layer of glue or paste on the 1/4-inch border of one of the sheets of construction paper and attach the two sheets together.
8. Individuals or pairs may exchange the Advent calendars they have made as gifts to each other, or they may use them as gifts for others, such as baptismal sponsors, shut-ins, friends, grandparents, etc.

Worship (5–10 min.)

Close by singing along with or listening to "Prepare Ye the Way of the Lord" from *Godspell,* or by singing together the following words to the tune, "O God, Our Help in Ages Past."

With joy and gladness in my soul
   I hear the call to prayer:
"Let us go up to God's own house
   And bow before Him there."
We stand within your sacred walls,
   O Zion, ever blest,
Wherein His people praise the Lord
   Their psalms to Him addressed.

They come to learn of Yahweh's will,
   Acknowledging His might
For there is judgment's royal seat,
   The kingly throne of right.
Because of friends and relatives,
   My heart desires your peace,
And for the house of God, the Lord,
   My care shall never cease.

(Words by James Montgomery, 1771–1854. Reprinted from *Extra Good News,* 1974. Franciscan Communications Center, 1229 S. Santee Street, Los Angeles, CA. Used by permission.)

Refreshments and Fellowship (20 min.)

For refreshments, you may wish to reflect food John the Baptist ate. If "chocolate-covered grasshoppers" are not to your liking, have some fruit or nuts, something natural—with water to drink.

Christmas Prayer

by Barbara Kloehn

Objectives

To discover and share what prayer is for us
To reflect on the prayers of others
To gain some insight into our personal and corporate spirituality and prayer discipline in the future
To pray

Materials Needed

> Paper and pencils
> Bibles
> Newsprint and felt-tip pen or chalkboard and chalk
> 150 to 200 small brown paper bags
> Several medium-sized pails of sand
> 150 to 200 3-inch votive candles
> 15 to 20 large boxes
> Several old cups or scoops

Introduction to Topic: And Then There Was Prayer!

It has always been there for us to use, to do. But how often we forget what power is ours in being able to communicate directly with our Creator. That's a big thing, and prayer becomes exciting when we realize its availability! We can pray anytime, any place, in any manner, and God has promised to hear. He has been doing that for generation upon generation, and He continues to be an omnipresent, listening Father for us now. Are we struck by the "power of prayer" when we think about its ever-present-employableness each day? But, of course, it is not prayer itself that has the power, but God Himself, who is all powerful and who listens to all who call upon Him!

Opening Activity (20 min.)

A. Ask each person to write down a word or simple phrase (usually what first comes to mind) to complete each of the following:

   1. Prayer is _____.
   2. The best thing about prayer is _____.
   3. Prayer is difficult when _____.

   The leader reads the beginning of these three sentences aloud, leaving 15 or 20 seconds after each for the participants to fill in the blanks.

B. Go around the group and have each person share what he or she wrote in response to number 1 and why he or she responded in that manner. If some have questions about certain responses, go back to those people after everyone in the group has given his or her answer. Then go around the circle a second time for responses to number 2 and a third time for responses to number 3.

This icebreaker is easily done in the large group. The leader, however, should be aware that "in depth" discussion may not happen at this point. Nor should it dominate this initial sharing time, when everyone should feel free and nonthreatened about his or her answer. All responses are valid in this exercise!

Bible Study (30 min.)

When we think of prayer, we often think of it as a way of asking God for something. But prayers also praise and thank God for what He has done, is doing, and will do for us. In this Bible study we will be looking at three prayers of praise and thanksgiving to God in Luke's gospel that are related to the birth of the Messiah. These three "Christmas prayers" are the Magnificat (Luke 1:46–55); the Benedictus (Luke 1:67–80); and the Nunc Dimittis (Luke 2:29–32). Begin this Bible study by making three columns on the chalkboard or on a sheet of newsprint with the headings "The Magnificat," "The Benedictus," and "The Nunc Dimittis." Beneath each heading write the verses in Luke where that prayer is found.

Divide those present into three groups. Ask the first group to look up Luke 1:46–55, the second group to look up Luke 1:67–80, and the third group to look up Luke 2:29–32. Each group should then answer the questions below about the prayer that has been assigned to the group. List group answers on the chalkboard or newsprint under the appropriate heading.

1. Who spoke this prayer?
2. What happened to bring about this prayer response?
3. What does the title of the prayer mean? (Each title is the Latin word for the beginning words of the prayer, for example, Magnificat: my soul "magnifies" or "declares the greatness" of . . .; Benedictus: "blessed"; Nunc Dimittis: "now let [me] depart.")
4. What kind of prayer is this?
5. List the verbs in the prayer. Identify the tense of each verb listed as past (p), present (pr), or future (f). Identify the verbs that express people's actions (P), and the verbs that express God's actions (G). What do these verbs tell us about the prayer?
6. Define the meaning of some of the verbs in their context, for example, what does it mean for God to "regard" in 1:48? to "visit" in 1:68? to "have prepared" in 2:31? Define the meaning of other verbs in the prayers.
7. Write a sentence or two that summarizes the content of the prayer.
8. When do we still use these prayers today? (The Magnificat is used in Vespers, the Benedictus in Matins, and the Nunc Dimittis in the Divine Service with Holy Communion.)
9. What brings about this prayer response on our part?
10. What is the meaning and purpose of the prayer as we use it today? Can we still identify with the meaning and spirit of the prayer? Why or why not?

Preparation for Worship (10–15 min.)

Give each person a slip of paper. Write on the chalkboard or on a sheet of newspaper, or have duplicated on 8 1/2" x 5" sheets of paper the following beginning phrases for three short prayers:

Adoration

Praise to You, O God! You are/have _____.

Intercession

Please, dear Lord, help _____/forgive _____/be with _____.

Thanksgiving

Thank You, Father, for _____.

Ask each person to complete the phrases to make three short sentence prayers. Collect the papers, cut them to divide the prayers into the three categories, and choose three people to share these prayers with the group during worship.

Worship (15–20 min.)

Create a worship atmosphere by lighting candles. Have several minutes of silence for private prayer and meditation before you begin the worship activities. You might go into the church sanctuary for your worship and sit on the floor in the chancel area in front of or around the altar.

Singing is most appropriate in a "prayer service," for to quote Martin Luther, "Music is the highest form of prayer." So begin your worship activities by singing an appropriate Advent or Christmas hymn. If time permits, locate in *The Lutheran Hymnal* or *Lutheran Worship* the prayers from Luke's gospel that you discussed in your Bible study and sing these, too. Have the three persons previously chosen read the prayers group members wrote. First, have the prayers of adoration read; second, the prayers of intercession; third, the prayers of thanksgiving. After each group of prayers is read, ask for any additional prayers. Close with the Lord's Prayer.

Project (30 min.)

Task

To make outdoor luminaries for your church's Christmas Eve worship.

Purpose

Besides providing pretty decorations for your congregation's and community's Christmas Eve celebration, these luminaries are symbolic of the light that shone round the angels on the first Christmas night and of how God's Son broke into the darkness of our lives with the light of His love to save us. These luminaries can be a great witness to you, your congregation, and your community as they point to Him who is THE LIGHT OF THE WORLD!

Method

1. Using old cups or small scoops, pour one or two inches of sand into 150 to 200 small brown paper bags. Put the bags into boxes for carrying.
2. On Christmas Eve, place the sand bags 4 or 5 inches apart along the driveway to your church, along sidewalks, on the sides of your church steps—anywhere where people will see them as they come for worship and where they can be seen by the surrounding community.
3. About 45 minutes to a half hour before your congregation's Christmas Eve worship, set a 3-inch votive candle deeply into the sand in each bag and light the candles. (*Note:* Be sure to have someone standing by with a garden hose or pails of water to protect against the possibility of starting a fire.)

Afterglow (20 min.)

Serve light refreshments, such as popcorn, Christmas cookies, and punch.

Day by Day: O Dear Lord, Three Things I Pray
(An Epiphany Night)

by Phyllis Kersten

Objective

To help youth gain a new understanding of regular private devotions (spiritual reflection and prayer) as an ongoing "Epiphany journey" through which they as young wise men and women will be enabled day by day

      to see Christ more clearly
      to love Him more dearly
      to follow Him more nearly

Materials Needed

    Bibles
    Construction paper
    Duplicated discussion questions
    Newsprint
    Magic markers
    Newspapers and news magazines
    Glitter and glue
    Stapler
    String

Icebreaker/Get-Acquainted Activity (30 min.)

Divide the total group into small groups of five to six youth. Each of the small groups has the same assignment: to discover as many things as possible that all members of the group have in common. The group should not list the obvious "commonalities" (i.e., goes to the same church or high school, has blue eyes) but should ask one another questions to find other less obvious things everyone in the group has in common. These can be things about their families or themselves, serious or humorous commonalities.

After 15 to 20 minutes, members of each group should report back to the full group what they discovered they had in common. The leader should note commonalities among groups and mention how an activity like this is a little bit like an Epiphany journey of discovery in that it reveals areas of commonality or interconnectedness—common joys or sorrows—with others that we were not aware of before.

Bible Study: Day by Day, an Epiphany Journey (30 min.)

Explain to the youth that tonight's focus is on private worship. Often we think private devotions are composed only of prayers and praise. Mention that tonight we want to broaden our understanding of private worship to see that

> it begins first with reflection—on Scripture, on Christ, on world events, on our own daily lives, on the needs of family and friends;
> it also includes bringing everything to God in prayer; and
> its ultimate purpose is an ongoing Epiphany journey of discovery—revealing our "interconnectedness" and commonality with Christ and with the needs of people around us.

Most of the youth present will probably recognize that tonight's theme, "Day by Day, Three Things I Pray," is a song from the musical *Godspell*. And they can probably supply the three main parts of the night's Bible study, taken from the song:

1. To see Thee more clearly.
2. To love Thee more dearly.
3. To follow Thee more nearly.

Mention that these are three specific goals of regular private prayer and reflection that we want to explore this evening on our "Epiphany journey," using the story of the wise men and of Jesus Himself as our guide. Divide the group into three small groups. Each group will take one of the three sections, explore it, and then report back to the larger group on what its members discovered on their "Epiphany journey."

Group A: To See Thee More Clearly

1. Ask the group to turn to Matt. 2:1-12, silently read the story of the three wise men, then discuss the following questions:
    a. What was it that led the wise men to the place where the Christ Child was (v. 2, 9-10)?
    b. The purpose of setting aside a regular time for private prayer and meditation—whether it's daily or weekly—is to reflect on the various "stars" or "lights"—in the created world, in personal or world events, in Scripture—that lead us to "see" God "more clearly." Can you recall an instance when something in nature, in God's good created world, led you to "see" God "more clearly" and worship Him in awe and wonder? Have there been particular world events, or events in your personal life that have led you to "see" God and His gracious intent for you and all people "more clearly"? Are there favorite Bible passages or events in Christ's life that enable you to "see" Him "more clearly"?
2. Have the group turn to Matt. 25:31-40, read the passage silently, then discuss these questions:
    a. According to this parable of Jesus, where can we "see Christ" today? What are some of the "stables," the common, out-of-the-way places, the "Bethlehems," where the Christ Child lies today?
    b. Part of our private worship should be a regular prayerful reflection on the needs of

those close to us as well as those around the world (we can get in touch with their needs through sensitive listening to TV news, reading newspapers and magazines, etc.). From this week's news, where can we see Christ "more clearly" in the needs of hurting people?

Group B: To Love Thee More Dearly

1. Ask the group to silently read Matt. 2:1–12, and then discuss these questions:
   a. How did the wise men worship Christ and express their love for Him (v. 11)?
   b. Verse 11 says that when the wise men opened their "treasures or treasure boxes," they gave Christ gifts. Sometimes we have trouble getting our various "gifts" or "talents" out of the "treasure boxes" that contain them. But in response to regular prayer and meditation, God will help us identify, "unwrap," and give to Christ our unique gifts.

   What are your gifts of "gold"—the best or most precious gifts or talents that you have? Do you have other gifts—a gentle smile, a good ear for listening, dependability—that might be more like "frankincense"—not as substantive as "gold," but like a pleasant scent or fragrance that might gently enrich other people's worship of God. The gift of "myrrh"—because of its use in embalming—can symbolize, in a sense, "gifts" of sorrow and suffering. Do you know instances where people have turned a personal sorrow or family tragedy (an illness, a handicap, a problem) into a "gift of myrrh," a gift that enables them to understand and help others with similar problems? What sorrow or suffering in your life might, through private prayer and reflection, become "a gift of myrrh," a gift that might help you be sensitive and respond to the needs of others?

2. Have the group turn to Matt. 25:31–40, read the passage silently, then discuss these questions:
   a. According to this parable of Jesus, how can we worship Christ with our gifts of gold, frankincense, and myrrh? How can we use our gifts to love Him more dearly?
   b. What are some of the specific needs of people—in the world, in our community, among our family and friends—that can be brought to Christ?

Group C: To Follow Thee More Nearly

1. Ask the group to silently read Matt. 2:1–12, then discuss these questions:
   a. What did the wise men do after they had found the Christ Child and worshiped Him (v. 12)?
   b. Is there a sense in which once we have been baptized and come to worship the Christ Child, we like the wise men return home "another way"? What is that "other way" (see John 14:6)?

2. The following passages suggest some of the things involved in journeying home through life "another way"—some clues from Christ Himself about what it means to follow Him more nearly.
   a. Read Mark 1:35; Mark 6:45–46; Luke 5:15–16. Following Christ more nearly means setting aside some solitary time for _____.
   b. What is "fit" to bring to God in prayer? Only our feelings of worship and praise? Or? See Luke 22:39–46; Matt. 27:45–46. Following Christ more nearly also means _____.
   c. Private prayer and meditation can sometimes be a "mountaintop experience," enabling us to see Christ in all His glory (see Luke 9:28–35). What were the disciples tempted to do with that mountaintop experience (v. 33)? Instead of prayer being an end in itself, however, it should lead us into following Christ more nearly down "on the plain," in the real world. What does that mean? See Matt. 25:32–40. Following Christ more nearly means _____.

Creative Activity (30 min.)

After group members report back briefly on what they've found on their "Epiphany journey," explain the evening's creative activity. From the materials available (see above), each person can choose to make one of the following creative projects:

  A. A meditation journal or devotional booklet to use in private worship. The individual should create the title pages at the youth night and then fill in the other pages during his or her daily or weekly private devotion times. The devotional journal might be titled, "Day by Day, Three Things I Pray."

Possible page titles under the three major headings might include the following: Under "To see Thee more clearly" could be included seeing God "more clearly" (1) in nature; (2) in world events; (3) in my daily life; (4) in special Bible passages; (5) in special worship services and youth activities; and (6) in the needs of people—family, friends, community, and world—today. Under "To love Thee more dearly" could be included (1) my gifts of "gold" that can be used to "love Christ more dearly"; (2) my gifts of "frankincense"; (3) my gifts of "myrrh"; and (4) the special needs of family and friends—opportunities to "love Christ more dearly." Under "To follow Thee more nearly" could be included (1) following Christ by bringing all of my needs and feelings to God in prayer, i.e., my temptations—the "cups" I'd like to pass from me; my disappointments—the times I feel "forsaken" by God and other people; my "mountaintop experiences"—my special joys, my spiritual "highs"; my feelings of weakness and inadequacy—when I feel I only have meager resources; and (2) following Christ by bringing the needs of others "down on the plains"—where Christ calls me to follow Him—to Him in prayer.

Explain that the three main section headings and the page titles can be written, "glittered," or illustrated with appropriate magazine or newspaper headlines or photos. Mention again that the actual pages of the journal will be filled in by the individual at home in his or her regular private prayers and reflection times by putting the date and a brief entry on the appropriate page.

B. A prayer poster—to take home as a reminder to set aside regular time, daily or weekly, for private prayer and reflection. Based on the evening's theme, "Day by Day, Three Things I Pray," the poster should use magazine photos, etc., to express visually the highlights of what it means to see Christ more clearly, to love Him more dearly, and to follow Him more nearly.

C. An Epiphany journey map. This spiritual map for wise young men and women of today should again visually convey the highlights of tonight's learning activity and through the creative use of photos, map names, glitter, and the like could include the following:

1. A section of the map labeled, "to see Thee more clearly," that has
   various places named (stables? countries? towns? jails? retirement homes? rural routes?) where we "see Christ" today in the needs of people;
   various wonders of God's created world (rivers, mountains, etc.) that enable us to "see Him more clearly"; or
   major events in our personal lives—events that helped us see more clearly God's gracious intent for our lives (e.g., our birth, baptism, hospital stay, etc.)

2. A section of the map labeled, "to love Thee more dearly," where the individual could
   draw a "Treasureland" or "Giftville" (a "Talentopolis"?) with some of his or her personal "gold," "frankincense," or "myrrh" gifts identified in boxes;
   draw roads from his or her gifts to some of the specific needs of friends and family or of hurting people in the community or overseas, etc.—where the individual is or could be using his or her gifts to love Christ more dearly.

3. A section of the map labeled, "to follow Thee more nearly." Like the wise men who came and worshiped Christ, we too, are "going home another way." The indiviudal should draw "home" (heaven? eternal life?) and "the way" (Christ), and some of the things he or she experiences along life's way. (Are there some mountaintop experiences? some valleys that have been "the pits"? some "Gethsemane" experiences? some "forsaken" hours?)

Worship (10–15 min.)

Sing the song: "Day by Day, Three Things I Pray."

(If there is time afterwards, you might want to sing one or more of the other songs from *Godspell*—for instance, "We Beseech Thee" or "All Good Gifts.")

Litany

Duplicate the following litany:

> **Leader:** Day by day, dear Lord, three things we pray:
> **Group:** To see Thee more clearly, to love Thee more dearly, to follow Thee more nearly, day by day.
> **Leader:** O dear Lord, we thank You
> **Group:** that we have come to see You as Savior, as the One who is with us in all of our lives.
> **Leader:** Dear Lord, we pray, help us this day . . .
> **Group:** to see Thee more clearly in the needs of our neighbor.
> **Leader:** O dear Lord, we thank You
> **Group:** that we have each been given special gifts—of gold and frankincense and myrrh—to worship You.
> **Leader:** Dear Lord, we pray, help us this day . . .
> **Group:** to love Thee more dearly by using all our gifts—to worship You and serve our neighbor.
> **Leader:** O dear Lord, we thank You . . .
> **Group:** for enabling us to return home another way—following Christ as the Way.
> **Leader:** Dear Lord, we pray, help us this day . . .
> **Group:** to follow Thee more nearly . . . in the practice of private prayer; in bringing all our feelings and needs to You—our hallelujahs and our hurts, our praises and our pain; in leaving the mountaintop to return to the plain, the plain old day-to-day world and service in Your name.
> **Leader:** Day by day, dear Lord, three things we pray:
> **Group:** To see Thee more clearly, to love Thee more dearly, to follow Thee more nearly, day by day.
> **All:** Amen!

Choose an Epiphany hymn for the closing song, for instance:
> "As with Gladness Men of Old"
> "Brightest and Best of the Stars of the Morning"
> "Songs of Thankfulness and Praise"
> "How Good, Lord, to Be Here"
> "We Three Kings of Orient Are"

Refreshments and Fellowship (20 min.)

Each person can create an ice-cream sundae "fit for a king" with various "gifts" brought by the youth: ice cream, chocolate, butterscotch, strawberries, nuts, whipped cream, etc.

If there is time for recreation after those ice-cream creations, the group might want to play a favorite from *The New Games Book:*

> "Aura," remembering that private prayer and reflection keeps us "in touch" with God and other people
> "Knots," highlighting again our interconnectedness through prayer with Christ and other people

It's Not Easy Being Green
(Each Person Is a Special Child of God)

by Terry Dittmer

Objective
That each person grow in awareness of his or her own unique self, of his or her specialness and individuality, especially as a child of God

Materials Needed
    Copies of the First Article of the Apostles' Creed with Luther's explanation (one for each person)
    Newsprint
    Green markers
    Personal inventory for each person
    Bibles

Introduction to Topic
Invite people to come dressed in green. Hang a poster of Kermit the Frog prominently. Decorate with green streamers and green balloons. As people arrive, give them green name tags or green necklaces—some sort of green identifying mark.

As the youth arrive, have each person create a newsprint self-portrait. Provide large sheets of newsprint and green magic markers. Ask each person to give some time to drawing himself or herself on the paper. Encourage the youth not to put down a circle face, dot eyes, and a line for a mouth, but to really try drawing themselves.

Arrange a portrait gallery along a wall. Have all persons view this collection of "art" as they might do if they were to visit an art gallery. You might want to have the "artists" suggest a price for their work of art, then notice the comments as the others respond to the worth of the pictures.

Devotion
Open with a song like: "Help, O Lord"; "Children of the Heavenly Father"; "Our God, Our Help in Ages Past"; "Amazing Grace"; "Psalm 40"; "Do Lord"; "Psalm 27"; or any song that reflects believers' dependence on God.

Read together Luther's explanation to the First Article of the Apostles' Creed.

Offer a prayer of thanksgiving for the persons present. Perhaps mention individuals by name in the prayer and mention something special about each person.

Study
Listen to a recording or sing your own version of "It's Not Easy Bein' Green." Check Sesame Street records or songbooks to get a copy of the song.

Bein' Green
    It's not easy bein' green.
    Having to spend each day the color of the leaves
    When I think it could be nicer being red or yellow or gold
    Or something much more colorful like that.
    It's not easy bein' green.
    It seems you blend in with so many other ordinary things
    And people tend to pass you over
    'Cause you're not standing out like flashy sparkles in the water
    Or the stars in the sky.
    But green's the color of spring
    And green can be cool and friendly like.
    And green can be big like an ocean or important like a mountain

Or tall like a tree.
When green is all there is to be
It could make you wonder but why wonder, why wonder.
I am green, and it'll do fine.
It's beautiful and I think
It's what I wanna be.

(Words by Joe Raposo. Copyright © 1970, Jonico Music, Inc. Administered by April Music, Inc. I-M-A. Used by permission.)

After listening to the record, discuss:
  What's the point of the song?
  When is being "green" good?
  When is being "green" bad?
  What's so hard about being a frog? (If the discussion needs stimulation, talk about frogs, bad press, warts, being slimy, weirdness, greenness, etc.)
  Have you ever felt "green"?
  Can you share a time when you felt totally different from the crowd?

"Green" is a word in the song used for individuality. In other words, Kermit is saying it's not always easy to be Kermit. Is it always easy to be you?

Give the youth inventory forms to fill out. Reassure them that they may keep their answers to themselves—they need not share them unless they choose to do so. Suggest they do this survey quietly by themselves. Read through the questions in case some clarification may be needed. Allow about 10 minutes.

Personal Inventory Form

1. Name: _____
   Do you like your name?
   Do you know what your name means? What?
2. What's your favorite color?
3. What's your favorite vegetable?
4. What kind of talents do you have?
5. What kind of hobbies do you have? What interests you? What do you collect?
6. What's your favorite book?
7. What's your favorite movie?
8. How do you feel about being male or female?
9. What's your favorite Bible verse?
10. What's your favorite thing about God?
11. How do you usually feel in the morning?
12. What do you think your parents think about you?
13. List one thing you like to do with people.
14. List one thing you like to do for people.
15. What is something about yourself you don't like?
16. What is something about you people like? (If you don't know, ask them right now.)

(Leader, feel free to edit, change, add to, or subtract from these questions. For question 1, have a name dictionary handy. In question 4, encourage each youth to discover his or her talent. Don't let the youth say, "Nothing." For instance, neatness, baking a cake, choosing coordinated clothing, smiling, etc., can be listed as talents.)

When everyone has finished the survey, ask how individuals feel about themselves. Pick out a few questions to discuss. Be sensitive to the fact that not all will feel comfortable with sharing every answer. Ask, "Is it ever a problem being you?"

Then read the following to the group.
  It's not always easy being me.
  I'm too fat . . . too skinny . . .
  I've got pimples . . . short hair . . . ugly hair . . . greasy hair . . . split ends . . . no hair at all.
  I'm a goody-goody . . . I'm not good enough.
  I'm too chaste . . . I'm too bad.
  I'm too honest . . . too obedient . . . too dishonest.

I've got no talent, and nobody notices me . . . I've got too much talent and everybody's jealous.
I'm too obnoxious, loud, and overbearing . . .
I'm too shy, too quiet . . . and boring.
I'm a wallflower, and I hate myself.
My clothes are too old.
My parents live in the dark ages and want me to live there too.
My parents are too much like me and try too hard to be "with it."
I'm not a part of anything . . . I'm apart from everything.
It's hard being a boy . . . being a girl.
To kiss or not to kiss.
To tell or not to tell.
It's not easy being me.

Talk about the reading. Reflect on the extremes. We tend to think about ourselves at one extreme or another on the personality scale. We may think we have absolutely no talent when, in reality, one person may like our cheerfulness, another our courtesy, and another our ability to entertain small children. In other words we may be the last to appreciate who we are and what we can do.

We may have our laments about our self-image like our frog friend, but stop and think about Kermit. Really, everybody likes him—he's not an ugly green toad but a celebrated celebrity. He's a celebrity because he is unique. He is himself. He is green.

So are we—we're special in our individuality, unique in our "greenness." Our uniqueness is all the more special because of our relationship to God. Think again about the First Article of the Apostles' Creed. How are we made? See Gen. 2:7 and 1:26-27. What do these verses mean to us individually? Who put us together the way we are? See Ps. 139:13-14. Who cares about us? How does God feel about us "nobodies?" See Ps. 145:15-16; Matt. 10:29-31; Ps. 37:4-5; 103:13.

When you feel down on yourself, what do the following verses say to you? 1 Cor. 7:7; 1 Peter 4:10; Rom. 12:4-8; 1 Cor. 12:4-7.

When you feel out of it—very green—how can the words of 1 John 3:1-3 help? In His grace, love, and mercy, in His forgiveness, God touches His children and makes them His. They are not "green" in terms of ugly, but "green" in terms of unique and special. To use the frog image, God kisses His children with love in Christ, ugly frogs that they are, and changes them into beautiful people, handsome princes and beautiful princesses. It may not always be easy being you, but God's there and cares.

That's something to celebrate . . . and to remember when you're down on yourself. God loves you . . . you're green, and that's great! Try singing "It's Not Easy Bein' Green" together, celebrating the fact that each is green in his or her own special way.

Recreation

Try a few frog-oriented games and activities like the following:
Leap frog
Kermit the Frog look-alike contest
Catching "flies" (black jelly beans) with your tongue
Musical lily pads (leaping from pad to pad till the music stops)

Make up frog jokes (example: Did you hear about Martin Luther Frog? He came from Wartburg).

Refreshments

Set a banquet table with green table clothes, green candles, green napkins, and the like. Then serve anything green, such as:

Green velvet cake (white cake with lots of green food coloring)
Green tea	Green peas
Green punch	Frog cookies or cupcakes
Lime sherbert	Lettuce
Green mashed potatoes	Cucumbers
Green beans	Frog legs

Family "Is Shoes" (Issues)
(Strengths and Weaknesses Within One's Family)

by David Schaefer

Objectives

To help participants recognize the individuality of family members (both their gifts and shortcomings)

To help participants celebrate and anticipate those times when the family is gathered together under the grace of God

To help participants appreciate more deeply those occasions when "family shoes" walk together

Materials Needed

Shoe boxes or grocery bags
Newsprint or chalkboard
Materials for recreational activities

Get-Acquainted Activity: Cinderfella

As participants arrive, secretly ask each one to remove his or her shoes and deposit them in shoe boxes (or grocery bags). Leave boxes unidentified. Leaders should sort guys' and gals' shoes into two separate piles. After the entire group has arrived, ask the guys to sit on chairs in a row while randomly giving each of the gals a shoe box containing one pair of unidentified shoes. Without help from the guys, gals are given 30 seconds to open, examine, identify, and put the shoes on the right owner. If a particular guy is chosen more than once, he will have to wear the extra pair(s) of shoes on his feet, hands, and ears. When finished, determine which gal "shod" correctly and award prizes, like shoe laces, shoe polish, and socks. Repeat the exercise in the same way for the guys so that they have the chance to find out to whom the "mystery shoes" of the gals belong.

Topic

People show great interest in their shoes nowadays because they wear them for more than comfort or protection: shoes have become specialty items. The idea of having special shoes for special reasons has been "soled" to the public. Shoes just for jogging, for basketball, for running, for decks, and other activities have made brand names like Adidas and Nike household words. Take a historical look at the shoes you're wearing.

> How old are they?
> Where did you purchase them?
> Why did they attract you?
> What special places have you worn them lately?
> What's the estimated mileage on your shoes?

List all the different kinds of shoes you can. Here's a sample list for starters:

running shoes	wingtips	oxfords
flip-flops	hiking boots	clogs
cowboy boots	loafers	safety shoes
moccasins	high heels	sneakers

Pick a pair of shoes to describe each member of your family. For example if you have a brother that just sits around watching television you might choose a "loafer" for him. Pick a shoe for yourself, too! What kind of shoes live at your house? Have the youth share in small groups.

Shoes symbolize family and family life. In the morning we put on our shoes to walk around in the world of school, work, and play. For most of us shoes in a family come together under a table when we eat our evening meal. After supper we kick off our shoes and relax before turning in. Family members allow us to take off our shoes, take care of cuts and bruises, and get ready for another day of traveling on.

The Scripture gives us a picture of a special family, the Livingstones. Read together 1 Peter 2:4–10.

To what does Peter compare Christ in verse 4?
Who should live their lives together?
What did Jesus call Peter once? (Matt. 16:18)
Do you think Peter remembered this when he wrote these passages?
What does building a "living house" mean?
Have you ever thought of your home as a "living house"?
Look at verse 9. Examine the special words Peter used to describe the church. The people in your family are also chosen . . . royal . . . holy . . . belonging to God . . . called to declare His praises.
What were some of your best times as a family?
Where were you?
What were you doing?
What made you feel good about it?
In verse 10, what special "gift from God" is available to make a family a family?
Why do families need this "gift" from God?
How do families experience this gift?

End by developing something participants can do with their families that's connected with shoes or stones, for example, they could take a hike together, start collecting rocks from places they've been together, go shopping, build a rock garden, etc.

Worship

A. Song: "Let Us Ever Walk with Jesus" or a similar "walking song"
B. Scripture Reading: Eph. 2:14–22
C. Litany for the Christian Family

Leader: Lord, bless our family . . .
Response: We need one another; we love one another; we forgive one another. We work together; we play together; we worship together. Together we use God's Word; together we grow in Christ; together we love all people; together we serve our God; together we hope for heaven. These are our hopes and ideals, help us to attain them, O Lord.
Leader: Lord, bless our family with openness
Response: to real communication.
Leader: Lord, bless our family with the ability to share
Response: all our joys and sorrows.
Leader: Lord, bless our family with freedom
Response: to let each other grow.
Leader: Lord, bless our family with understanding
Response: for the gifts each one has to give.
Leader: Lord, bless our family with love
Response: no matter what, no matter where.
All: Amen.

D. The Lord's Prayer
E. Closing: Close with another "walking song," such as "Just a Closer Walk with Thee."
F. Benediction

Recreation

Game 1: The Oxford Puppet Theatre

Have available a generous amount of magic markers, cardboard, yarn, glue, scissors, and cloth. Divide the group into smaller groups of three or four. Each group will design puppets by decorating the soles of their shoes and then putting them on their hands. Treads make interesting texture.

Ask each group to write a script, using the puppets, for the members' own production of *My Fair Sneaker* or other musicals and plays. Each play should last three to five minutes and will be judged on the writers' ability to play on "is shoe" phrases. Examples: "I'd like to leave, but I'm tied up just now." "Why do you want a box of concrete for Christmas?" "'Cause I'm really into 'sole' food." "I'm usually a solo performer, but I'm forced to work with this loafer."

Appoint a panel of judges to select the best performance and award prizes to top playwrights.

Game 2: The Great Race

Youth should pick partners and then form teams with four people in each team. On all fours (hands and knees) each player should tie one lace on one shoe to the lace on the other shoe. Then the lace that is nearest to his or her partner's should be tied to the partner's closest shoelace. Clogs may require string.

If all goes well, there will be four people in a row with eight shoes tied together. All four place their hands into the shoes and at the signal race toward a goal. Everyone must remain on hands and knees. (*Hint:* The racers may soon discover that they go faster at a walking pace, rather than trying to hop.) The winning team is the one with the best time.

Refreshments and Fellowship

Try serving "sole" food or food connected with shoe images, for instance, "shoefly" pie, shoestring potatoes, chicken wing-tips, or fillet of sole. Or use recipes from the *Complete Book of Jogging*.

Barefootin' and Carefootin'
(Appreciating Our Family)

by Lavern Kruse

Objectives

To develop more sensitivity to our families' needs
To recognize that we need our families' caring concern
To appreciate our families and the unity that holds us together
To develop greater appreciation for God's love as expressed through our families

Materials Needed

A clay vessel
Modeling clay for each person (about the size of a golf ball)
A Bible for each participant

Introduction to Topic

Our individual personality and life-style are shaped by our family environment. God has given each of us specific talents and gifts. We also have certain weaknesses because of our own sinfulness. Our lives are like clay—events occur that crumble our dreams and our hopes rather quickly. As family members, we reach out to one another, and we strive to reshape our shattered world. Our family should be people to whom we can expose our clay feet and receive comfort and healing.

Setting

Choose a setting where youth can shift easily from the whole group into small groups. Try to meet in a room where an altar can be the focal point during the worship event. Consider having the worship in church before God's altar.

Just for Fun

After the youth arrive, display a clay vessel of any size or shape and ask each person to guess its weight. (Be sure you know what it is!) Announce the winner later in the evening. Offer a small gift item made from clay to remind the winner of this event and of his or her place in God's world as related in tonight's activity. If your budget is limited, consider asking local restaurants for free gift certificates.

Opening Remarks

Briefly describe the objectives for the night's events.

Icebreaker (20 min.)

Divide the participants into groups of six or smaller and have them form a circle. Give each participant a piece of modeling clay and ask him or her to mold a form or shape symbolic of a positive experience or event that occurred within his or her family this past week. After 10 minutes, allow individuals to share their symbols in that group for approximately 1 1/2 minutes. The person with the largest shoe size should begin. The group members should place their symbols in the center of the circle as they share their experiences and then leave them there to be used later.

Scripture Study: A Strong Body with Clay Feet (30–45 min.)

Have the entire group study Dan. 2. (The leader should study this chapter in advance and share the highlights of the chapter so the group can concentrate on verses 31 to 45.)

As we discuss this passage, we learn that the massive idol in Nebuchadnezzar's dream crumbled, symbolizing the triumph of the kingdom of God fulfilled in the coming Christ. This account assures us that God is the Ruler and Caretaker of all—and that includes each of us today. We should be reminded often to seek God for our source of strength. While Daniel pictures the crumbling of the Babylonian and Persian empires by the crumbling of the large idol, this picture can also illustrate human weaknesses. We find strengths and weaknesses in our entire family, even our parents. All of us have clay feet. We need to tread softly with one another in certain aspects of our lives. Sometimes our clay feet are crushed, and we need someone to put them together again. Our home should be one place where we, relying on God as our source of strength, can reach out to piece together our broken feet. What role do you play in this process with your family? What role does your family play when you need help? Explore this further with the following activity.

Exposing Our Clay Feet and Strong Body

Instructions: Have youth move back to their original groups of six or less. Have three persons sit on three chairs with their backs together in a triangular shape. The other three group members should set their chairs facing the three center chairs. See illustration. (If groups are smaller, devise a system to exchange seats.) After each of the following statements has been discussed, the outside person should rotate one chair to his or her right to share with other individuals. Read each statement and answer several statements before asking the group to share. Allow approximately two minutes of discussion between each statement.

1. The person in my family whose feelings are hurt the easiest is . . .
2. I get hurt the easiest when . . .
3. My parents seem hurt when . . .
4. My brother or sister is hurt easily when . . . (If you have no brother or sister, share something about someone who is close to you.)
5. A real strength in my character is . . .
6. A real strength in my parents' lives is . . .
7. A real strength in the life of my brother or sister is . . .
8. The greatest strength in my family as a whole is . . .
9. The greatest weakness in my family as a whole is . . .

Discuss the following statement in your group of six: If I could suggest one thing that could draw our family together more closely in Christ, I would suggest that we . . .

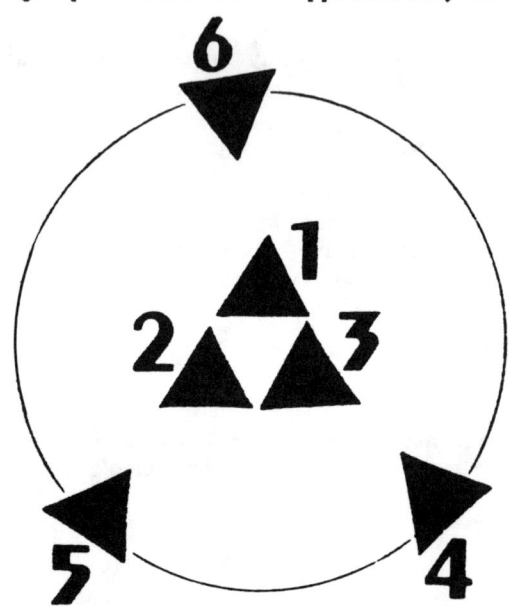

As a group, take your clay symbols and combine them into one large ball. Mold this large piece of clay into a group symbol that incorporates the ideas expressed in the last statement.

Worship (15 min.)

Gather the group together in an open-ended circle with the altar at the open end for the focal point. Light the altar candles and lower the room lights for a more worshipful atmosphere. Ask members of each group to bring their symbol to the worship area.

Invocation

    Leader: In the name of the Father,
    Group: who created our entire being,
    Leader: and of the Son,
    Group: who takes our clay feet and heals them when they're broken
    Leader: and of the Holy Spirit,
    Group: who gives us power and strength to reach out to others, especially our families, as we live our daily lives.
    All: To Him be the glory and honor, forever and ever. Amen.

Song

"Here We Are" or "Thank You"

Sharing of Symbols

Have each group share what its symbol means. As a pledge of the commitment to work together toward the goal set for their own family, have members of each group place their symbol on the altar. (Be sure to place waxpaper or protective covering under the symbols so that the altar will not be damaged.)

Sharing Scripture

Read Ephesians from *Epistles Now* by Leslie F. Brandt, keeping in mind this evening's discussion in reaching out to our families.

Closing Song and Prayer

To symbolize their willingness to reach out to those in their family whose clay feet may crumble, have youth reach out now to one another in the group. Have them do this by standing up and grasping their neighbor's hand. If group members feel close to each other, try a circle hug but leave it open-ended to allow the focus to still be on the altar.

Sing "They'll Know We're Christians by Our Love."

Prayer: Allow individual responses of thanksgiving or petitions to be expressed. If your group feels uncomfortable doing this, the leader should be prepared to have a closing prayer based upon some thought expressed during the evening's study.

Recreation (20 min.)

To reinforce the evening's theme of being sensitive to one another's needs and reaching out to help one another, arrange an activity that demands the support of each person in the group. Begin with your groups of six and build pyramids. Be creative in designing new forms and combinations. Combine groups for building larger pyramids. Then end with one big pyramid with everyone in it, on it, or under it.

Afterglow

Have youth go in pairs for refreshments, each person picking up the food for his or her partner. Partners could even feed each other if they like. Encourage them to share some difficulties involved in reaching out to others.

Remember to announce the winner of the guessing contest.

The Shoelace Acceptance—Do It Now!
(Worth of Individual Family Members)

by Keith Oetting

Objectives

To provide activities for family units that demonstrate and build the worth of individual members
To demonstrate that building self-worth is important and should be practiced now

Materials Needed

    Bible study sheets
    Pencil
    Paper
    Tape
    Blindfolds

Background

This program provides a balance between input by the facilitator and activities by the participants. Where these guidelines suggest input, the facilitator will want to explain and adapt them for his or her own style.

Planning

Emphasize that this youth night is designed for families and that all parents are invited, making clear that parents will participate in a relaxed, nonthreatening set of activities.

Gather together Bible study sheets, pencils and paper, and tape, then blindfold each participant. Make sure transportation is available for each family. Have enough sandwiches and drinks for everyone. Each family should bring a can or two of its favorite soup. Find a large cooking pot, one you estimate will hold all the soup being brought.

Time and Place

Plan to spend three hours in a church basement or fellowship hall that has a kitchen. Set up tables to seat three or four, allowing space between each, rather than arranging in long rows.

Introduction

Shoelaces symbolize things we need and receive from our families. Just as we learn to tie our shoelaces at home, so we learn other functions, traits, and needs from our families. Virginia Satir, a prominent family therapist, claims that the single most important thing that children learn from their families is a sense of self-worth. American ingenuity has found replacements for many needs, but not for God's gift, the family.

Many of the emotional problems that crop up in life are connected to low levels of self-esteem. The best way to build up self-worth in an individual is to verbally communicate acceptance and appreciation. This is true for children as well as teens and adults. We learn our self-worth by being accepted and appreciated by others, especially our families. Paul, in Rom. 5:8 tells us that God loved us while we were still sinful. Parents too can express unconditional love and acceptance of their children, and children can express unconditional love and acceptance of their parents.

Arrival—"Goup Soup" (10 min.)

As participants arrive, ask them to carefully mix their soup into the pot with everyone else's in order to make "goup soup." The soup can be cooking during devotions. Encourage an informal and relaxed atmosphere by playing some background music.

Devotion (10 min.)

Ask each family to be seated at one of the tables. Welcome family members and introduce the theme for the evening. Explain the objective for the evening and the symbolism of the shoelaces. Talk about the importance of building self-worth in individual family members. (For help see Virginal Satir, *Peoplemaking*, chap. 3, "Self-Worth: The Pot Nobody Watches." The chapter is only nine pages long. Your library or mental health center should have a copy.)

Have someone read Rom. 5:8 and explain that because God loved us while we were still sinful we too can express unconditional love, regard, and acceptance for others. Close with a prayer and ask everyone to join in a table prayer.

The "Goup Soup" Meal (30 min.)

Serve soup and sandwiches to everyone cafeteria style, but encourage families to eat together. After the meal discuss the great strength of the family in years past when family members worked together on a farm or in a small family business. Ask family members to clear off their tables together, but don't have anyone wash the dishes yet.

Icebreaker (15 min.)

Have a family scavenger hunt. Each family should sit at its own table. As you read off the items, one family member races to get the item to you first. Possible items might be a driver's license that expires this year, a shoelace, a sock with a hole in it, a social security card with number 4 on it, a library card, a belt, a wedding band, a comb, a strand of brown hair, a barrette, a ball of lint, a credit card, a hairpin, a doctor's appointment card, a business card, a hunting or fishing license, Certs, a hairbrush, or a $2 bill.

Warm-ups (15 min.)

After everyone has returned to his or her table, the facilitator should explain that the group will do some verbal exercises to help everyone express appreciation to each other. Each person must invest hard work, openness, and honesty in these exercises. Each person's attention should be centered entirely on his or her own family. Tell individuals to concentrate on what their own family says and does rather than trying to impress other groups.

Before doing this exercise, encourage some warm-ups. Have everyone write on a piece of paper his or her answers to these four questions about the 20th century.

1. Who was or is the most important person?
2. Which person has done the most harm to humankind?
3. Which man has brought the most humor into the world?
4. Which woman has brought the most humor into the world?

Then have each family member share his or her answers to the first question. After discussion, do the same in order with the other questions. The facilitator should give examples of some answers and explanations. Give encouragement to families and compliment them on the warm-up exercises.

In-Depth Study (60 min.)

Ask the families to imagine that in exactly one half hour everyone in the family will loose his or her sense of sight. Ask: "What things would you like to see for the last time?" Tell the families that in exactly one half hour everyone will be blindfolded for the rest of the activity.

Give each family a few minutes to decide what its family members want to see during their last half hour of sight. Have them get into their cars and go see it. Most people will probably go home to see other family members. If people live too far away from church, suggest that they go to a nearby park or to a relative's home. Impress on them that they have only 30 minutes.

Everyone should physically move as a part of this excercise. Family members may just want to look at each other, but encourage some physical effort. Allow time to clarify instructions and then send the families on their way.

When the people return, blindfold them, and take them to their tables. Ask them to imagine that in 10 minutes they will lose their ability to speak. Then tell them that in 10 minutes everyone will have a piece of tape over his or her mouth and will no longer be able to see or speak. Tell them you will read two sentences, allowing each person time to complete each sentence for every other member of the family. Read these statements and then suggest some possible responses.

1. One quality or characteristic about you that I really appreciate, but have never told you about is _____.

2. One thing that you have done or still do that I appreciate but have never told you about is _____.

Allow a few minutes for people to prepare answers (no talking allowed during this time) and then give them only 10 minutes for sharing. Tell the families when their time is about up and at the end of 10 minutes give everyone a piece of tape to place over his or her mouth. Allow participants to sit in the dark and silence for awhile. Then say, "If seeing the members of your family was important enough to you that you chose to be with them during your last half hour of vision, why wait until the end to do it? If seeing family members was that important to you, why not spend some quality time with each other every day? And if there were things about each other that you appreciated, but waited until now to say, why not say these things when you can, when they have meaning for you life?" You may want to remove the participants' masks in order for them to discuss these ideas.

Break (10 min.)

Bible Study: 1 Cor. 12:14–26 (30 min.)

Ask everyone to return to his or her family group. Again, compliment family members on their hard work and ability to share. Hand out Bible study sheets printed with 1 Cor. 12:14–26. Have someone stand to read these Scripture passages. Everyone should read through the Scripture, putting question marks by passages he or she does not understand and underlining passages that have great personal meaning. Everyone should share his or her feelings in his or her family group, taking care to explain passages with special meaning and to attempt to answer someone else's questions. The facilitator should help with unanswered questions.

Ask each family to determine what this Scripture implies about Christian families and write down its response. Allow no more than 15 minutes for this entire exercise.

The remaining 15 minutes should be spent paraphrasing the Scripture to show that each member of the family has something valuable to offer to the others. Encourage creativity. The verses need not be followed exactly. Suggest that the word "family" be inserted wherever "body" appears and that names of family members be inserted where body members are mentioned. Suggest that individual qualities of family members be inserted where body part functions are mentioned. Form is not important so long as each family member and a quality of his or hers is mentioned. Give some examples, for instance, verse 15: "If Dad says, 'Because I am not a mom, I don't belong to the family,' . . ."

Goup Soup (5 min.)

Ask the entire group to consider what goup soup teaches about families. Stress that no matter how hard we try we could never create a combination like the one tonight. No two families are alike, and each soup contributed something to make the end result what it was. So, too, does every member of the family contribute something. Though each can of soup seems to lose its identity in the "goup soup," family members do not lose their individual identity.

Closing

Ask each family member to write down something he or she learned during the evening and some activity members can do at home to encourage them to express appreciation of each other. Close with a prayer asking for the power of the Spirit to continue the work begun.

Shoes . . . I Know Where You're Coming From
(Empathy in Relationships)

by Ben Freudenburg

Objectives

To examine the role of understanding and compassion in helping us become better friends
To help us to be more sensitive and caring to the other person's circumstances

Materials Needed

- Colored paper
- Pencils
- Newsprint
- Bibles
- Tape
- Magic markers
- Scissors
- Tape measure

Introduction to Topic

"You don't understand! You just don't understand!" The words are familiar. We may have spoken them at one time or another. Certainly the words speak a common frustration. Whether the relationship is teen to parent, spouse to spouse, or friend to friend—in truth, often we do not understand what the other person is feeling, experiencing, or thinking. And our lack of deep understanding may lead to broken communication, rejection, and real pain.

"Walking a mile in another's shoes" is more than a simple attempt to understand what his or her life is like—more than an exercise in sympathy. Among people who know each other well, the "shoe exchange" must be an attempt to go beyond sympathy to empathy. Empathy is "feeling with" another person. It is sharing an experience or emotion so completely that real understanding of "where the other person is coming from" emerges.

Such empathetic communication is rare, and it is difficult to create. But it is the core of Christian relationships that go beyond acquaintance, even friendship, to the kind of healing community that can foster spiritual and personal growth. It is toward such empathetic relationships among Christian teens that we move with this youth night event.

Icebreakers

1. Divide participants into groups of 9 (or multiples of 3 up to 15). Use colored sheets of paper to represent each group. Ask participants to stand on a piece of paper, trace around one of their shoes, cut out the tracing, and tape it to themselves. Arrange participants into groups by color. Ask them to join hands, form a circle, and sit down.

    Give these directions: Take your shoes off. Each group is to build the tallest freestanding tower of shoes. I'll give you 10 seconds to plan and, on the command to begin, 20 seconds to build.

    Make sure you have a tape measure to find the winner. If your group has nine or fewer members, do the exercise three times and see if you can improve the height each time.

2. On a piece of newsprint in a shoe outline write out the following sentence stems and questions.

    a. I bought this shoe . . .
    b. The choice was . . .
    c. I chose it over . . .
    d. I bought it because . . .
    e. How does this shoe reflect your personality?

    Ask participants to complete the sentence items on the "shoe" they traced and cut out.

    After five minutes or so, ask groups to share all of the items. The person with the smallest shoe goes first, then the person to the left goes next, and so on in turn around the circle. As you give instructions, you might review "rules for listening": good eye contact, complete attention, etc.

Learning Activity

While group members are sharing, take a shoe from each person in each group. Keep the group's shoes together. Before the next exercise, be ready to distribute group A's shoes to group B, group B's shoes to group C, etc. After everyone has shared, give one shoe to each person and move into triads.

This activity is to help us become more sensitive to others' circumstances. Even though we might not like the shoes others have on or the people in them, how did hearing some background and reasons for the purchase of the shoes help you to be more accepting of the shoes? of the person who owns the shoes? Let's move one more step and look at the role of compassion in friendship. Really get to know the shoe in your hand. Try to understand it by answering these questions:

1. List three places the shoe has been and explain how you know (e.g., classroom, gym, field, etc.).
2. If the shoe could feel, what primary feeling would it have? What caused that feeling?
3. The shoe has an owner; tell how the owner feels toward the shoe at this moment. Why?
4. How does the shoe feel towards its owner?
5. Give the shoe a name—a real name. Give the shoe personality by using an adjective that begins with the same letter as the name does, for example: Snappy Sam, Hurting Henry. Let the name reflect your understanding of the shoe.

Share about the shoe in triads:

Round 1—A shares; B listens; C observes
Round 2—B shares; C listens; A observes
Round 3—C shares; A listens; B observes

Roles

The sharer has three minutes to explain his or her understanding of the shoe.

The listener listens, and after the sharer is finished, takes one and half minutes to tell the sharer what has been said.

The observer has two minutes to evaluate the listener and share observations about the owner of the shoe.

After sharing, discuss this question: "How does knowing where a person has been and understanding what he or she feels help us in our relationship with this person?"

Bible Study: "The Compassion of a Friend"

This Bible study lets us see Jesus interacting with His friends. Give each triad one of the following three friendship situations: Peter and Jesus, Judas and Jesus, Mary and Jesus.

On newsprint, display the following three sheets:

Peter and Jesus	*Judas and Jesus*	*Mary at Bethany and Jesus*
Describe friendship	Describe friendship	Describe friendship
Mark 14:27–31	Matt. 10:4	Luke 10:38–42
Matt. 16:13–20	John 12:1–7	John 12:1–3
John 21:15–19	Mark 14:10	
Describe problem	Describe problem	Describe problem
Matt. 26:69–75	John 13:26–30	John 11:28–44
Explain how understanding leads to compassion and forgiveness.	How did understanding lead Jesus to compassion?	Explain how Jesus' understanding led to compassion.

Each group is to analyze Jesus' action in the friendship situations by looking up the passages and answering the three questions. After the triad has finished, ask members to note their responses on newsprint. Then discuss each situation.

To conclude, discuss this question: "How can understanding and compassion help each of us as we deal with old friends?"

List answers on newsprint.

Recreation

Shoe Relays

Teams stand single file facing a chair several yards ahead. Each person takes one shoe from the person ahead, and the first person in line (who has been given the shoe of the last in line) sits on the chair. At the start the new first person in line runs, kneels, and puts the shoe he carries on the person in the chair (then ties it) and sits in the chair when the person with two shoes returns to tag-start the next participant. Winners get all of their shoes on first.

Variations: Put the teams' shoes all in a pile between the chair and team. This time the participants have to find the right shoe first! If competition isn't a good idea, make the whole group one team. Use a stop watch to try to improve your time.

Shoe Toss

This is a variation of Egg Toss. Try it using hiking shoes, cowboy boots, and the like.

Shoe Grand Prix

Two teams sit in a circle, determine the number of laps, and see which team can complete the race (pass the shoe) first. Add sound effects and rules: Every other person must hold the shoe, or it starts at the beginning; if the shoe has a wreck (it drops), you must start over, etc. Try a figure eight. Try to race with a shoe marked by a yellow ribbon. Obstacles, such as the chairs for tunnels, can also be added.

Worship

Ask the members of the original groups of nine or more to find each other, hold hands, and sit down with knees touching. Put a bunch of small slips of paper in the middle of each group with some pencils.

Read 1 Peter 2:2–3 aloud and join in singing several favorite hymns or songs. Then ask everyone to take off one shoe and put it in front of him or her. Participants are to use the slips of paper to fill the shoes with good things about the owner of the shoe. Write good characteristics, talents, a memory, etc., on the pieces of paper. After everyone has finished stuffing the shoes, have a time of silence as each reads what the others have offered.

Repeat this prayer aloud:

We are God's,
*   and He made us with good things.*
He understands us
*   and still loves us.*
Hold us tight, Lord Jesus.
*   Help us to love each other as You love us.*

Afterglow

Fill each shoe with good things, such as hard candy, suckers, tootsie rolls, etc.

Careful Saints
(People Who Care)

by Dennis Hintz

Objectives
That the participants may understand caring as an essential characteristic of Christian community
That participants may rejoice in their place as "God's own people" individually and in community

Materials Needed
Chalkboard or newsprint
Bibles
Candle

Introduction to Topic

Within each repetition of the Apostles' Creed we affirm that we are "in this together." We believe in "the holy Christian church, the communion of saints." In the Large Catechism Luther describes this "communion of saints" as a "holy communion" into which the Holy Spirit leads us by Word and Sacrament.

First Peter 2:9–10 tells us that as members of this "holy communion" we are "a chosen race, a royal priesthood, a holy nation, God's own people, that [we] may declare the wonderful deeds of Him who called [us] out of darkness into His marvelous light. Once [we] were no people but now [we] are God's people; once [we] had not received mercy but now [we] have received mercy" (RSV). Think of this wonderful news and rejoice: "God's own people!" He has reached down in love and graciously and mercifully chosen us to be His very own.

As His own, "holy community," we are to "declare the wonderful deeds of Him who called [us]." Notice also the plural emphasis: we are not alone but in community.

Our God-made community is founded on Jesus Christ (1 Cor. 3:11), and the love (agape) that sets us into special relationship to God is the same love we share with others who are His own. We do not create love for one another, but as we mirror God's love to one another, we are enabled to be "CAREful Saints."

Icebreaker (15 min.)

Form a tangible community using a game called "Knots" (from *The New Games Book*). First ask the participants to gather shoulder to shoulder in a circle. Then everyone reaches into the center of the circle and grabs a couple of other hands. Instruct participants to avoid the hand of someone right next to them or both hands of another person. Shift or switch until "knotted" into one large circle (or two interconnected ones) of people with joined hands. Do this without breaking handholds. Hands should not be entirely released, but a light grasp may eliminate bends, breaks, or bruises. A round of applause is in order when the knotty problem is completely unraveled.

Ask participants to try to remember some personal observation and impressions during the untangling that can be shared later. (*Special Note:* 6 to 16 persons can be involved in each "knot"; the more people, the more difficult that task.)

Bible Study (60 min.)

Divide participants into groups of four to six persons.
1. Caring and care can have many meanings. Write some or all of the following on the board or newsprint. Ask participants to choose the item that comes closest to their understanding of the basic meaning of "care."
    a. "Cares of the world."
    b. "I really care about this job."
    c. "I care about you."
    d. "I'll take care of you."
    e. "Be careful."

After each person has chosen a response or two, break into groups of three to four to share selections. A brief explanation for selections may also be shared.
2. The passages listed below are several that deal with caring. Ask each participant to read two or three of the passages silently and determine what aspect of caring is highlighted in the text. After about 10 minutes for reading, each participant may share the insights within the small groups. After 10 more minutes, ask each group to report some of its insights on the Biblical view of caring. Note some of these on the board or on newsprint.

Rom. 12:6–8	Rom. 12:10	Rom. 12:13
Rom. 12:15	Rom. 12:18; 14:19	Rom. 13:10
Rom. 14:1	Rom. 14:7–8	Rom. 15:1–2
Rom. 15:5–7	1 Cor. 12:12, 21, 25–26	1 Cor. 16:17–18
2 Cor. 1:3–7	2 Cor. 8:1–2	

3. Read John 11 aloud. Then ask the small groups to discuss the chapter, using the following statements and questions, which you might reproduce on the board.
   a. List those who cared for others. List those who needed care.
   b. Each participant should identify the character in the chapter that seems most like himself or herself. These can be shared as well as the reason for the choice.
   c. In your opinion, which character was the most caring? the most cared for? the one needing the most care?
   d. What do you think were the greatest needs of Mary? Martha? Lazarus? Jesus? the disciples? the Jews (v. 33)? the chief priests and Pharisees?
4. Ask each person to select two or three of the items below and prepare responses for discussion. Allow 15 minutes for the sharing. You might ask the small groups to report some of its learnings and insights.
   a. Describe several situations when caring is not really caring. What determines when an actor is really caring?
   b. Why do some people resist being cared for? What reasons can you list? How can some of these reasons be overcome?
   c. List five persons who care about you. Share about one or two of these with the group. Tell how and why their caring was special to you.
   d. Without using names, recall a recent situation where you cared for someone else. Describe the person's reaction and yours.
   e. Make a list of five personal needs to which you would like someone to respond. Share one of these with the group if you desire.
   f. Identify and share one way that this small group could respond directly to you.
   g. As a caring person yourself, what gifts or talents do you have that you would share with the other members of this group who may desire and need your care?
5. As a closing activity for this study, turn to John 10:10–11, 14–16, 27–28 and read the verses out loud together. Then as you have time, discuss this question, "How do these promises fit into our discussion this evening?"

Worship (15 min.)

Have the group sit in a circle. Place a cross and lighted candle in the center to symbolize the presence of Jesus, who "cared" enough for us to give Himself into death. For that reason we are His own; we are called out of darkness into His marvelous light. You might make a personal comment on these truths and ask others to comment.

Join hands and sing "Blest Be the Tie That Binds."

Close with this blessing:

> Now may the God of peace who brought again from the dead our Lord Jesus, the great Shepherd of the sheep, by the blood of the eternal covenant, equip you with everything good that you may do His will, working in you that which is pleasing in His sight, through Jesus Christ, to whom be glory for ever and ever. Amen. (Heb. 13:20–21 RSV)

Afterglow (15 min.)

The entire group may wish to try the Knots game again to see if it can be done in less time and with more cooperation.

Light refreshments may be served. Encourage those who have become aware of someone's specific need tonight to respond with care to that need.

Footsteps and Footprints
(Following in Jesus' Steps)

by Mikell Peratt

Objectives

To examine where we have been and where we are going as servants (followers) in Jesus' footsteps

Materials Needed

Large sheets of newsprint or wrapping paper
Felt-tip markers
3" x 5" cards
Advent wreath or log
Matches
Bibles
Paper for drawing
Slips of paper with Bible verses for worship
Songbooks or hymnals
Cutout cookies
Frosting tubes
"Sock" for recreation

Arrival (20–30 min.)

Use large sheets of newsprint or wrapping paper to cover an entire area on the floor. Place an Advent wreath or Advent log in the center of the newsprint. Ask each person to trace his or her footprints twice, anywhere on the newsprint and facing any direction. One set of footprints represents where the person has been; the other represents where the person is going. If time allows, have participants decorate each set of their footprints with symbols or pictures of where they have been and are going.

After each person has added his or her footprints, ask the group to sit down around the newsprint. Ask each person to share something about his or her two sets of footprints. Discuss the following questions.

1. What direction are the footprints going?
2. Whose footprints are close together or off by themselves? Was this accidental or deliberate?
3. Are all the footprints going in the same direction, or are they going in many directions? What does this say about our group?

Discussion (30 min.)

A. Footprints and footsteps represent growth.
   1. Pass around 3" x 5" cards, each having one of these statements on it:

      first-step footprints   first-step at school
      learning-to-run footprints   moving shoes
      running-away-from-home shoes   lost shoes

    new shoes
    sport shoes
    dating shoes

    biking/hiking shoes
    driving shoes
    no shoes

    You may add other statements, leave some cards blank, or repeat some for a large group. Have enough or more than enough cards for the people present.

    Ask each person to choose (or to draw) a card and then to share some feelings about that "footstep" in his or her life.

    Have each person share these events by saying, "I'm wearing _____ shoes (footprints), and I feel _____ because . . ."

2. Now pass around another set of cards and do the same type of sharing about the stages of spiritual growth:

    Baptism shoes
    Sunday school shoes
    VBS shoes
    Confirmation class shoes
    Confirmation Day shoes
    slippers for family devotions

    church shoes
    acolyte shoes
    bare feet at summer camp
    choir shoes
    witnessing shoes
    Holy Communion shoes

B. In what direction are you walking?

1. Have participants list places where their footsteps take them each day. After individuals do this on paper or verbally, you might want to write all the places on a chalkboard or a piece of newsprint for all to see.
2. Read Luke 9:23–26.
   a. Jesus says we are to deny ourselves, take up our cross daily, and follow Him. What does this mean in your daily life?
   b. If you did as Jesus commands, what footsteps in your life would be different?
   c. What footsteps would probably be the same?
   d. Where might your footsteps go that they don't go now?
3. Read 2 Cor. 5:18–20.
   Jesus gave new direction to our footsteps. Now we are to share that new direction with others.
   a. What kind of footsteps does an ambassador make? Are they his or her own footsteps or someone else's?
   b. How would being an ambassador for Jesus change your daily footsteps?
4. Read 1 Cor. 12:4–11.
   God gives each of His followers a gift or several gifts to be used to equip the saints (those who follow Jesus) for the work of ministry, for building up the body of Christ (us followers).
   a. What gift(s) has God given you? Take off your shoes and cut or draw a symbol or picture to represent your gift(s). When you are finished, place your shoes in front of you, pointing toward the Advent wreath or log.
   b. Go around the circle and have each person share his or her gift(s) as he or she shows his or her symbol or picture. Then ask the rest of the group to call out ways in which that gift can be used to follow Jesus and to help the whole body of believers in their growth.

Worship (10–15 min.)

(Pass out these Bible passages to several people beforehand and ask each one to read them at this time.)

1. Our footsteps in this world, as human beings, begin in darkness. (*Dim lights.*) This darkness represents sin, our natural state. The darkness of sin makes it impossible for us to reach out to others, to walk together.
   Read 1 John 2:11.
2a. But God knew our needs, and He sent Light to our darkness. (*Light the candles as the next two Bible verses are read so that the room grows gradually lighter.*)
   Read Is. 9:2 and Luke 1:76–77, 79.
   Sing "Walkin' in the Light."

OR

2b. We are called to put on our shoes and to take footsteps into the world—to go out and be Christ to others. Read 1 John 1:5, 7. We need each other's help if we are to be "lights" in our world. Join hands and ask each person to pray a sentence for the person on his or her right.

Sing one of the following:
"Hand in Hand"
"Through the Night of Doubt and Sorrow"

If we are to follow Jesus, we have to put on our shoes and GO. Have each person put on his or her own right shoe, silently asking Jesus to direct him or her. Then ask each person to assist a neighbor in putting on the left shoe to symbolize our helping each other.

Recreation (30 min.)

Follow the Leader

Line up in one long line. If you have a very large group, you may need to make several lines. The first person in line leads the line around the meeting room or the entire church building, if it is available, doing various actions. Each person in line, as he or she comes to that place, duplicates the leader's action (following in the leader's footsteps). You may want to change leaders occasionally.

Walk a Mile in My Shoes

Divide into two teams, each team sitting in a row of chairs, side by side, facing the other team. Choose the person with the largest feet to sit at the right end of each row. Each person removes his right shoe and places it under his chair, except for the person on the far right, who keeps his or her shoe on. At the word "go," this person runs around the back of his or her team's row of chairs to the other end. Meanwhile, everyone on the team moves up one chair so the chair at the left end of the row will be empty. The person wearing the shoes sits down, removes his or her right shoe, and passes it up the line. Each person must pass the shoe (no tossing)! When the shoe reaches the person now at the head of the line on the right, he or she must put the shoe on, run around the line of chairs, sit down, remove it, pass it, etc. The team that finishes first after every person has worn the shoe and the shoe's owner is once again wearing it and sitting at the head of the line is the winner.

Whose Shoes?

Ask the group to sit in a circle, with one person as "it" in the center. Each person takes the name of a different brand of shoes (e.g., sneaker, loafer, moccasin, Adidas, etc.), calling it out for everyone to hear. No two persons may have the same name. One person in the circle begins by calling out the name of his or her shoe and the name of another shoe. The person whose name was called must repeat his or her shoe name and the name of another shoe before "it" can hit him or her with the sock. (Use a long sock with its mate tucked into the toe.) If a person is struck before calling the name of another person's shoe, he or she is "it," and the former "it" sits down and begins the game again. A person may not call the name of the person who just called his or her name, or the name of "it's" shoe.

Refreshments and Sharing (10–15 min.)

Ask someone to make a large batch of cutout Christmas cookies ahead of time. The cookies may be in Christmas decorations, gingerbread people, or in the shape of feet or shoes. Place frosting decorator tubes and other sprinkles and decorations on the table with the cookies, and have each person decorate at least two cookies—one to eat himself or herself and one to share with someone else.

Stress and School

by Steve Sonnenberg

Objectives

Identify individual causes of stress in school life
Identify signs or symptoms of stress
Learn how to be a support for persons under stress

Materials Needed

Yellow, green, pink, blue, and white cards or pieces of paper (enough so each person has one)
A name tag for each person (for use in the Trading Card Game)
Chalkboard and chalk or newsprint
Markers
Tape
Three pieces of paper for each person
Popcorn popper, popcorn, butter, salt, cider, or hot chocolate

Icebreaker: Trading Cards (30 min.)

Divide into two, four, or more equal groups with five persons in each group. (If your group is too small, the subgroups may have as few as three or four in them.) Give each member an envelope containing five trading cards (one yellow, one green, one pink, one blue, one white) and a name tag with the name or the symbol of his or her group. Ask group members to wear their name tags on their chests.

Post and discuss the rules of the game.

1. Each trading round lasts three minutes. There will be four rounds.
2. Participants who wish to bargain must stand facing each other.
3. There is absolutely no talking except while bargaining.
4. Once players begin to bargain, a legal trade must take place (two cards of different colors must be swapped).
5. Only one-card for one-card transactions are legal.
6. Players may indicate that they choose not to trade by folding their arms across their chests.
7. Players may not show their cards to anyone, with the exception of the one card they are trading to another player.
8. At the end of the game each player will calculate his or her individual score. The team score is the total number of points held by each player.
9. Cards values: yellow, 50 points; green, 25 points; pink, 15 points; blue, 10 points; white, 5 points. In addition, bonus points are awarded for holding three or more cards of the same color. Three cards of the same color are worth 10 points; four, 20 points; five, 30 points.

    For example, the score of a hand of three blue cards and two yellow cards is 140 points: three blue at 10 points equal 30, plus two yellow at 50 equals 100, plus a bonus of 10 totals 140 points.

The leader announces the beginning of the first three-minute round of trading as soon as the teams have had a chance to plan their strategy. After each round the teams have four minutes to plan their strategy for the next round. At the end of the four, total the scores and award a prize to the winning individual and team.

Discussion (30 min.)

This activity is designed to cause some stress on individuals as they work to succeed individually and as a team. In many ways this depicts existence at school. There are many times when the stress of surviving as an individual is challenged with the stress of surviving as "one of the team or group." Make a list (on the board or newsprint) of the stresses felt while playing the Trading Card game.

Post or reproduce and hand out the following list of Signals of Stress in an individual:
1. Disregards low priority tasks
2. Reduces amount of time given tasks
3. Tries to avoid responsibilities
4. Blocks out new information
5. Is only superficially involved; appears to give up
6. Negative attitude
7. Appears depersonalized or detached
8. "Going by the book"—centered on following the rule no matter what
9. Is overly precise or intellectual
10. Displays inappropriate humor
11. Breaks the rules to get even with the institution or leader
12. Wastes time
13. Is late or absent

Using this list as a basis for identifying stress in someone's life, go through the items one at a time, asking group members to share the degree to which they felt themselves experiencing each signal of stress during the Trading Card game. They should rate their identification with the signal on a scale of 0 to 10 with zero equaling no identification. Discuss how this affected their participation in the game.

Look again at the list of Signals of Stress. On a sheet of paper have each person write down the name of a school friend or acquaintance (or two or three) who exhibits each stress signal. Participants may also leave various "signals" blank if they do not know someone who fits.

Supporting Each Other (30 min.)

In many cases of coping with stress people most need to know that they have a friend who cares and will support them. This next activity is designed to help participants practice supporting others and to feel the effect of being supported by others. Have the group sit in a circle. Each person takes a turn, going around the circle stopping in front of every other person, looking at him or her, and saying, "You are . . ." (complete the sentence with a positive comment about that person).

As soon as the person going around the circle has made a positive comment, the recipient responds with the same comment. (For example, the person in the center says to A, "You are helpful," and Person A replies, "You are helpful." The center person goes on to Person B and says, "You are pretty," and Person B responds, "You are pretty," and so on. Continue until everyone has had a chance to be the one walking around the center. Finally, discuss how it felt to hear those nice things.

If it wasn't a good experience, try to determine why. What was stressful about this activity? Discuss how positive comments can be helpful to people at school who are stressed—specifically, those people whose names are on their list of Signals of Stress.

Bible Study and Worship (30 min.)

Look at Jesus' account of how to deal with anxiety (stress) as it is reported in Matt. 6:25–34. Don't worry, Jesus says, about your life, what you should drink, what you should eat, your body, what you should wear, or even about what's going to happen tomorrow.

Regroup into the same teams that worked together during the Trading Card game and come up with examples of the stresses at school that are associated with each of the areas that Jesus says we don't need to worry about: (a) our life, (b) what we drink, (c) what we eat, (d) our body, (e) what we wear, and (f) what's going to happen tomorrow. Share the results of these lists with the whole group.

Think of examples of positive "You are . . ." statements that could be used to help a person who might be trying to cope with a stress mentioned in each of the "no need to worry" categories.

Conclude the Bible Study and Worship by having each person write on the front of a 3" x 5" card a statement that says something about stress and anxiety in his or her life at school. Collect the cards, shuffle them, and redistribute them, being sure no one gets his or her own card. Write a prayer on the back of the card asking God to bless this person in the special way necessary to deal with the anxiety or stress mentioned. Take turns reading the front of the cards and the prayer that has been written as a special response to that need. Have everyone join in the Lord's Prayer, which reminds us of God's care for us during all times of stress.

Recreation

A fun, active, and affirming game would be in order for this evening. It is called Shuffle Your Buns. Arrange chairs in a circle so that everyone has a chair. Two people volunteer to go to the middle of the circle, leaving their chairs vacant. The persons sitting in the chairs keep moving around from chair to chair to prevent the two in the middle from sitting down. If one or both of the two in the middle manage to sit in a chair, the person on the right of these individuals replaces them in the center and tries to sit in an empty chair. (If your group is small, you may want to have only one person in the center and only one vacant chair.)

Refreshments

This active game will surely stir up thirsts and appetites. Bring a corn popper from home and make a batch (or two) of popcorn and serve apple cider or hot chocolate.

Good Grief?

by Paula Mott Becker

Objectives

To help youth accept their own feelings
To talk about stages of grieving
To provide help in moving through stages of grief
To help youth live with loss

Materials Needed

> Pieces of paper
> Bibles
> Chalkboard or newsprint
> Chalk or markers
> Refreshments

Introduction to Topic

The process of grief is sometimes a very long and painful journey. The pain is often associated with a loss in our lives, from a move away from a loved one to the permanent separation of death. The loss does not need to be great and devastating for grief to occur. We deal with losses in our everyday lives and, to some degree, we experience grief.

Opening Activity: Feeling Charades

As participants arrive, give them a piece of paper with one of the following feelings words on it: joy, fear, excitement, frustration, anger, hope, loneliness, disbelief, hatred, love. (Feel free to add to this list.)

If your group is large, not all participants will receive a word. They will help to guess what feeling is acted out.

Explain that the feeling words must be acted out. Those acting out the words must attempt to visually depict a person experiencing that emotion. They may use objects or even another person, but they may not speak while they relate the word. The group should be seated so that all can see and guess the word. When the group has guessed correctly, the word should be written on a chalkboard or newsprint for later reference. Do this with each word.

What Do I Do with My Feelings?

Divide into groups of four or six. Have each person choose three words from the list made during the feeling charades. For each word, have participants complete the following statement: "When I feel _____, I usually . . ." Each person in the group should share his or her response. Take time to discuss these questions:
1. What reactions seemed to help in dealing with specific feelings? Why?
2. What reactions are possibly harmful? Why?

When Loss and Grief Occur—How Do I Cope?

(Before the following experience, prepare group members by telling them about the importance of listening and being sensitive to the speaker's feelings.)

1. If possible, ask a congregational member who has experienced grief to come and share with your group. Meet with the person prior to the youth night and make your expectations clear. The person should have completely worked through the grief process and be able to talk freely about his or her doubts, frustrations, and anger. The individual should not necessarily tell all the details of his or her experience but rather discuss the stages he or she went through in learning to cope with the grief. The participants should understand that those stages and feelings are important and necessary if we are to conquer the giant called grief. Our despair, questioning, and feeling of rejection are not necessarily signs of weak faith but part of a process that God graciously allows in order to help us work through the difficult and painful experiences of life.

    Time should be allotted to discuss the presentation. (*Note:* The above experience is preferred because it allows young people to become directly involved with a real experience of grief and gives opportunity for the speaker and the young people to minister to each other as they listen, learn, and respond in care and acceptance.)

    If it is not possible to have a speaker, gather participants in a circle and ask them to list some experiences in life that cause them to grieve. Identify death, divorce, loss of friends, or family through such an experience, and ask them to talk about it if they wish. Someone may know of another person's experience and could tell about that. (If individuals are open enough to discuss their grief, the leader should help the group to listen and to accept what is said. Judgment and evaluation should not be part of this discussion.)

2. Ask the group to reflect on what was said and list the feelings and emotions that people have when they grieve. Write them down on newsprint. Help group members to discover the following:
    a. Shock/Disbelief—"How can this be happening to me?"
    b. Anger/Resentment—At the people involved in the loss, the loss itself, and at God.
    c. Despair/Depression—Loneliness and isolation.
    d. Panic—Inability to concentrate/preoccupation with loss.
    e. Guilt—"If I only had/or had not, then maybe this wouldn't have happened."
    f. Acceptance—"I can live with what has happened."
    g. Hope—"The future looks better—I can make it, and good things will still happen in my life."

    Spend time talking about the importance of people working through any or all of these stages, which are normal in adjusting to living with loss.

3. Now ask the group to write down some positive actions people can take as they work through grief. You might include the following ideas.
    a. Talk about the feelings you are experiencing. Express anxiety, anger, and frustration.
    b. Be alone when you need to, but accept the love and concern of those around you. Don't be afraid to go to them when you need comfort.
    c. Deal with the hurt by acknowledging your feelings but don't allow yourself to dwell on them.
    d. Select carefully those to whom you go for advice.
    e. React carefully and slowly after much thought.
    f. Do not be afraid to seek out professional help.

Into the Scripture

Divide into the same small groups as before. Read Ps. 142 together and answer some of the following questions.
1. What are the feelings the psalmist is expressing?
2. What does he want from God?
3. How does he feel towards God at this point?
4. Do you ever remember feeling that way about your life? When?
5. Do you remember feeling that way towards God? When?

Now read Matt. 11:28-30 and Prov. 3:5-6.
1. How could these words bring healing and help for the psalmist?
2. How can they help you as you face the struggles of life?
3. What are those words trying to tell us?

Worship and Celebrate

Sing together "No Longer Strangers." Gather in a circle. Ask someone to read the following poem slowly and expressively. Ask another person to lead the group in hand motions while the words are being read.

I See the Lord	**Actions**
I see, Lord, in my tightly clenched fists, The representation of myself; I hold onto myself, my cares, my possessions, my pride, and my hurts.	*Tightly clench fists and hold them out in front of you.*
I shut You out lest You change me. I shut other people out lest they would know me, lest they would hurt me. In fact, I could strike out with these fists against those who would threaten me.	*Bow heads and cover with open hands.*
But I see in the tight knuckles and tense forearms what this is doing to me. I am uptight, enslaved, imprisoned within myself: I am tired, tense, lonely, and in despair. I am only destroying myself.	*Bring arms up above head, clench fists, and look upward.*
And now, in slowly opening my hands, I release myself to You, Lord. Take my guilt, burdens, cares, emptiness, and loneliness.	*Slowly bring arms down and open hands.*

Stop reading and ask the group to share hugs, handshakes, and words of care and healing, for example, "You are important to me," "I love you," "God's peace be yours," or "God loves you, and so do I."

Get back into the circle and continue the reading.

My arms no longer hurt! My knuckles are no longer tight! Thank You for release, for freedom, for peace. With open hand I can no longer shut You out, shut out people, strike against those who threaten me.	*Slowly raise arms with hands open.*
Open hands are for helping! Fill them with Your love. Show them what to do, how to witness, how to serve.	*Bring arms down and keep them outreached as if holding something.*
Suddenly I am aware of the hurts and needs of other persons, other situations.	*Bring hands together and lift them to eye level.*

In my mind's eye I place them in these
   hands
and lift them to You for Your sustaining
   grace
and healing touch.
No longer alone, I reach out to clasp the
hand of brother and sister.
I thank You for him and her.
I pray for her and for him.
Shape us together into the body of Christ.
Amen.

Reach out and clasp the hand of the people on either side of you, keeping hands raised.

(Reprinted from "Balloons, Anchors, and Grappling Hooks," *Resources for Youth Ministry*, 71.4. Used by permission.)

Relax and Unwind

Make some popcorn, or if you have a fireplace, roast some marshmallows and have some soft drinks. A record or tape of some contemporary Christian music can play softly as you share refreshments and talk.

Called to Comfort

by Terry Dittmer

Objectives

To bombard youth with healing experiences
To equip youth to serve as healers in brokenness
To help youth identify a person or persons to whom to minister

Materials Needed

Puzzle pieces from want ads
Tape
White paper
Markers or crayons
Bibles
Copies of worship liturgy

Begin with a Puzzle Race

After your group has arrived, divide youth into teams of two or four persons. Give each team a puzzle that you have prepared beforehand. The first team to assembly its puzzle wins.

To make puzzles, take large sheets of colored posterboard or pages from the want ads of the newspaper. Cut these into puzzles of 30 to 50 pieces each. Each puzzle should have the same number of pieces and be moderately challenging. Straight-sided pieces cut at a variety of angles can be quite challenging. Estimate beforehand the number of persons you expect to attend the youth night and decide on the maximum number for a team. Give each team masking tape. The first team to tape the puzzle together and mount it on the wall is the winner.

Allow each group to finish. Finished teams become cheering sections. Encourage positive "cheers" rather than jeers and cynical remarks.

After the race, discuss the experience.

1. How did you feel about the pressure?

2. Did you work well together?
3. Note the masking tape "Band-Aids" and how they "healed" or "bound up" the "rifts" in the puzzles.
4. Reflect on the puzzle as a "bunch of broken pieces" put back together or "reconciled" with each other.

Personal Sharing

Have group members do some personal sharing about when and how they have felt like so many "broken pieces."

1. Draw out the discussion by giving each person a sheet of white paper and a marker or crayon. Ask participants to draw the following:
    a. a picture of brokenness;
    b. an expression of how they feel when they experience brokenness; or
    c. a response to brokenness as it exists in our world.
2. Encourage them to share their drawings.

Note: Some youth may not have experienced "brokenness" or may not want to reveal their own "brokenness." Be sensitive. Help them to respond, perhaps in terms of No. 3 above. Also be sensitive to hints that someone may need help and check on them later.

Bible Study

1. Summary: Brokenness is sometimes a part of our lives. Sometimes we need healing and reconciliation. Sometimes we need help.
2. As Christians, we know God Himself promises help and healing. Check out the following Scripture references. As you read them, share what they say to you. Make a note of words that describe God's relationship with us in our brokenness, words like faithfulness, reconciliation, comfort.

    Encourage the youth to react to God's help: How does it make them feel? How do they experience it? How do they know it exists? How do they respond to it?

    | Ps. 103 | Ps. 147:3 | 2 Thess. 3:3-4 |
    | 1 Peter 5:7 | 1 Cor. 1:4-9 | 2 Cor. 5:18-20 |
    | Eph. 2:19-20 | | |

    (On the last verse, you may wish to extend the discussion to include talking about the rights, privileges, and obligations of "citizenship," i.e., the support and care of the community.)
3. Read 2 Cor. 1:3-5 as a transition. Note that we are assured of God's comfort and called on to be comforters.
4. We are called to be comforters, called to be a community in Christ, encouraged to be God's "tools" or "agents" of healing to each other in brokenness. Have youth look up the following references and brainstorm how we all can be comforters or "Band-Aids" to each other.

    | Rom. 1:11-12 | Gal. 6:2 | Phil. 2:3-4 |
    | Eph. 4:31-32 | Col. 3:13 | Gal. 5:14 |
    | 1 Peter 3:8 | | |

5. Summarize by looking at Acts 2:41-47, the story of the earliest Christian congregation. What example for developing a "healing community" do these people give us? Look especially at verse 42.
6. Brainstorm what your group could do to become a more caring, supportive, healing community.

    Emphasize the need for this kind of caring and suggest asking for God's help and blessing. Then move into worship.

Worship

The worship is designed to be a relatively brief but potentially moving experience. The success of the worship is dependent on the group members' cooperation. Provide copies of the worship liturgy for each person. Have the group form a circle by standing shoulder to shoulder. Once the circle is formed, have each person take one step backward. A space of 12 to 15 inches should separate persons, but they should still form a circle.

Invocation

>L: In the name of the Father, the Son, and the Holy Spirit,
>R: Let us begin. Amen.

The Reading from God's Word: 2 Cor. 5:18–19

The Confession (in unison)

Dear heavenly Father, we live in a broken world; we see lives in pieces. We experience brokenness in our lives, and we sometimes do the breaking. We pray, O Lord, for healing and for reconciliation. Forgive us and put us together in Christ, who came that broken people might be mended.

The Assurance

>L: God has brought us to Himself. He continues every day to heal and comfort us. He cares for us in Christ Jesus. He loves and always will. Be assured in His love. Live in His reconciliation and be reconciled to each other.
>R: Amen.

The Charge: A Prayer of St. Francis of Assissi

Have one person read the prayer for the group:

> O Lord, make me the instrument of Thy peace,
> Where there is hatred, let me sow love;
> Where there is injury, pardon;
> Where there is discord, union;
> Where there is doubt, faith;
> Where there is despair, hope;
> Where there is darkness, light;
> Where there is sadness, joy;
>
> O Lord, grant that we seek
> not to be consoled, but to console;
> not to be understood, but to understand;
> not to be loved, but to love,
> For it is in giving that we receive,
> in forgetting that we find ourselves,
> in pardoning that we are pardoned,
> and in dying that we are born to eternal life. Amen.

Suggestion: Play "Peace Prayer" from the album "Come to the Quiet" by John Michael Talbot (Birdwing BWR-2019).

The Rite of Binding

This activity begins in the circle with the leader and moves clockwise to the leader's left.

The leader says: "Let us be bound to each other in Christ, caring and supporting each other, for His sake."

The leader places his left hand, palm down, on the right hand of the person to his left, also palm down. Using his right hand, the leader tapes their hands together at the wrist. Wrap tape around the wrist twice. The person on the left then tapes his or her left wrist to the next person's right until the whole circle is taped together. Be sure to have enough tape. (*Note:* An element of cooperation is necessary. The person taping has to "carry" the hand of the person he or she is taped to as he or she tapes himself or herself to another.)

The Benediction (in unison)

> May the Lord bless us and keep us.
> May He make His face to shine upon us and be gracious to us.
> May He keep us bound to Himself and to each other and give us peace. Amen.

Closing Hymn

> "Blest Be the Tie That Binds"
> "Will the Circle Be Unbroken"

Recreation

1. Build a "Human pyramid"—supporting each other.
2. Practice "first aid" carries, i.e., the fireman's carry.
3. Hold a piggy-back relay.
4. Finish with a giant group hug.

Refreshments

Build English muffin pizzas from scratch. Have all the elements that go into pizza available, i.e., English muffins, tomato sauce, sausage, pepperoni, green pepper, mushrooms, olives, etc. Have the group make pizzas for each other by "reconciling" the ingredients into a whole.

Success with a Capital "S"

by Miriam S. Meyer

Objectives

To help young people evaluate society's definition of success
To enable each youth to personally redefine success to include the idea of Christian saving grace and servanthood
To provide comfort and encouragement to those who consider themselves "losers"
To enable each young person to practice "serving" someone else

Materials Needed

> Paper
> Newprint
> Bibles
> Box

(*Note:* Keep the title and theme of this youth night a secret. Do not announce it to the group prior to the Bible Study.)

Warm-up (20–30 min.)

As youth and counselors arrive, have them write their first and last names on two pieces of paper. One piece goes into a box marked "Partner" and the other into a box marked "Password."

Explain that the group will play a verson of "Password" in which they will guess the name of someone in the group. Clues will be single words that describe the person: clever, smart, kind, athletic, spiritual, etc. Other clues may be a person's talents, interests, skills, physical attributes, etc.

Only positive and upbuilding characteristics are to be used. Negative comments will result in immediate disqualification. Avoid the use of nicknames or other obvious clues.

Begin with one volunteer or set an example by being the first to start. Here's how to play:
1. Pick a name from the "Partner" box. (If you pick your own name, replace it and draw again.)
2. Your partner comes forward and sits facing you.
3. Draw a name from the "Password" box. Let no one see it but you. (Use the name even if it is yours or your partner's name.)
4. Give one-word clues for the name. The partner responds with one guess per clue.
5. Allow one minute to complete the round. If the name has not been guessed, the audience may guess the name.
6. Continue around the group until everyone has a chance to pick from the boxes and give clues.

If the game is an emotional tension builder for the group, allow five minutes—no more—for a break. If individuals feel a need to ask, "Why did you use that word to describe me?" encourage them to do that now.

Bible Study (30–45 min.)

Recruit two volunteers to play one more round of "Password." Give one a piece of paper with the word "success" on it. The other person is to try to guess the word.

Also recruit a third person to record on a blackboard or poster paper the clues and responses in separate columns.

Allow one minute for the round. If the word has not been guessed, allow two other partners to try for another minute. Continue this procedure until the word is guessed.

After the word is guessed (especially if guessed quickly), have the entire group brainstorm other clues and record those on your list. Label that list "The World's Definition of Success."

Now prepare to make another list adjacent to the first and entitle it "God's Definition of Success." Have everyone look up one of the following Bible passages. Working individually or in pairs they should study the passage and jot down ideas on what the Lord apparently deems success.

Phil. 1:12–26	Matt. 6:19–21	Phil. 3:12–21
Gal. 5:13–14	Phil. 4:12–19	Ps. 100
James 4:12–19	Matt. 20:25–28	Luke 21:1–4
Rom. 12:9–11	Luke 18:18–30	John 13:3–15

The following rather detailed example could be given from Phil 1:12–26:
—being a servant of Christ
—giving others confidence in the Lord
—helping others witness more boldly
—preaching about Christ from genuine good will
—receiving help from the Spirit of Jesus
—being courageous in the Lord
—being in prison because of the Lord
—bringing honor to Christ
—living in Christ
—doing worthwhile work
—dying in Christ

After listing the idea under "God's Definition of Success" and comparing this with the list of "The World's Definition of Success," have everyone write a brief but specific paragraph entitled "My Own Definition of Success."

Worship (10–15 min.)

As you finish paragraphs, hand out song sheets and rearrange chairs in preparation for worship, then sing the opening song.

Song

"Spirit of the Living God"

Prayer

Dear Lord, we praise and adore You for Your incredible wisdom. We confess that our idea of success often has not been what You will for our lives. Thank You for sending Jesus to be born in a humble stable, to die on a rugged cross, and to rise from an earthly grave so we can experience the marvelous success of being in heaven with You. Help us to celebrate this success by helping and serving one another. Amen.

Song

"He's Everything to Me"

Responsive Reading

Ps. 23

Song

"Joy to the World"

Sharing

Provide opportunity for everyone to share his or her personal description of success.

Song

"Put Your Hand in the Hand of the Man"

Recreation

Volley Volleyball

Standard volleyball rules are used except that a team can score one to three points depending on how many times the ball is hit on its side of the net before sending it back. (If only one person hits the ball, one point is scored, if it is hit twice, two points are scored, and three points for three hits.) A game is 35 points.

Infinity Ball

Rules of standard volleyball apply except that the score, chanted aloud by both teams, is the number of times the ball goes over the net without touching the ground. Try to set your own group record and break it the next time you gather.

No Volleyball Net?

Try Hug Tag instead. Play as you normally would play tag, except the only time a player is safe is when he or she is hugging another player. For variety, make the rule that only three or more persons hugging are safe.

(Games are from *The New Games Book* edited by Andrew Fluegelman.)

Refreshments and Closing (10–20 min.)

As the group gathers, lead in a prayer of thanking God for the evening together, asking His guidance to view success from His perspective, and asking help to serve one another.

Divide the youth into two groups. The first group will serve refreshments to the other group, and the second group reciprocates. Serving should be done in the spirit of joy and honor and accepted with humble gratitude. (Washing one another's feet could also be included, but isn't absolutely necessary!)

My Success Goal

by Wendy Powell

Objectives
To help youth set some goals for their lives
To help youth evaluate their goals in light of their Christian commitment

Materials Needed
Puzzle pieces (pattern at right)
Newsprint or chalkboard
Markers or chalk
Sheets of paper
Pencils

Icebreaker

Superheros are all over these days. They range from He-Man and Mr. T. to Fernando Valenzuela. These characters and people have abilities that enable them to do what the average person is unable to accomplish.

As a get-acquainted activity, have participants think of their current heroes. Have them discuss who the person is and what attributes make the hero outstanding.

Learning Experience

Prepare the puzzle pieces ahead of time. (Either make a sheet with pieces to be cut out or cut them out yourself.) You will need to have one puzzle for each person.

Distribute the puzzle pieces and have everyone begin at the same time. Although there are only four pieces, the puzzle should be confusing. If you can, call "time" before anyone finishes.

At the conclusion of this exercise, participants usually will continue working. The goal becomes success. A simple four-piece puzzle cannot be that difficult! The prize in this contest becomes success.

This game is a small sample of the feeling that drives most of us toward success. Far too often, goals for success are set so high that we never reach them. We set ourselves up for failure from the beginning.

In this session we would like to take some time to honestly examine our futures in light of how God sees success and then set some goals toward that success.

Have the group choose three persons it considers to be successful. On newsprint or a chalkboard record the names and reasons for the responses.

In columns on a sheet of paper, have participants list the occupations that they have considered for themselves. (Include husband, wife, etc., as well.) Next have them circle the ones they consider to be the strongest options at this point in their lives. It would be best to circle no more than three options. Underneath each of the circled columns have students list (1) the things that make a person successful in these areas, and (2) things that could be barriers to success. For example:

Computer Programmer		Mother		Teacher	
1.	1.	1.	1.	1.	1.
2.	2.	2.	2.	2.	2.
3.	3.	3.	3.	3.	3.

Split into groups of four or five and have students discuss their responses. Don't spend too much time here, only enough for basic sharing. Discussion will come later.

As a group, read Phil. 3:4-6. List the marks of success that Paul shared in verses 5 and 6 on newsprint or a chalkboard. These verses point out that Paul was from the tribe of Benjamin, a good line of people, with the highest credentials as one of God's chosen people. He was a Bible scholar and defended the church to the point of putting dissidents to death. He obeyed the law to the letter. Now, read verses 7-11. They point out the perspective a Christian must maintain. Any success is "garbage" (TEV) without knowing Jesus Christ. Discuss why Paul could say that he counted his successes as loss without Christ.

Have the students look again at their lists in light of the following passages:

        1 Peter 4:10-11   Ps. 8   Phil. 3:12-16

A successful servant of God is one who lives in the world and does many jobs. At this point it is crucial for participants to see that whatever a person does, this is his or her work for the Lord, and it must be done in the attitude of Phil. 3:12-16.

As a concluding exercise, have the students complete the following sentence stems:

1. For me, success is . . .
2. The major goals I have for my life are . . .
3. In order to meet these goals I need to . . .
4. I will need God's help . . .
5. My family's support is needed to . . .

Worship

At this time of year we think of giving gifts to those we love. We have the assurance of success because of Christ. We have a purpose for every day.

In your group, take a moment to think and then respond to the following sentence stem, "If I could give Jesus a present, I would give Him . . ." (Any response, whether it be a costly gift or something intangible, is acceptable.) Share one at a time.

Have someone read Phil. 4:8-9 from a modern translation.

Close by singing some favorite songs of praise, such as, "Thank You," "Christ Is Changing Everything," or "He's Everything to Me."

Recreation

Invent some new rules for one of your group's favorite games so that no one can lose, or play the game "Twister" (available in many department stores). For an added "twist," have contestants make sure that no one fails!

Lusty Lady, Cradled Lamb
(Jesus' Love as Strength for Our Loving)

by Karen Melang

Objectives

To look at Jesus' unconditional love
To examine our relationships
To gain strength from Jesus' love so we may also love

Materials Needed

    Paper
    Pencils
    Baby pictures of participants
    Poster

Icebreaker (20 min.)

Use your local grapevine to request that people bring baby pictures of themselves. Ask that they bring pictures that can stay at church for a number of weeks, but assure them that the pictures will be returned (and make sure they are). Tell them *not* to share their pictures ahead of time with other people who are coming to this youth night.

Appoint someone to say hi to everyone who comes and to collect and number the pictures. This person may need an assistant to make up a master list of the numbers and names that go with each picture and to keep pictures in order. When everyone is settled comfortably, pass out paper and pencils and have the participants number their papers, one number for each picture. Begin passing pictures one at a time. The object is to guess the identity of each of the adorable little tots. (No fair giving yourself away by blushing at your own picture!) Read the list when all the pictures have been scrutinized by everyone. Who correctly guessed the most? Who has changed the most? Who looks most like they did when they were little? Who looks just like Mom, Dad, or siblings? Have people attach their baby pictures to a premade poster that looks like this:

(Poster illustration: a cradle with the text "CRADLED IN GOD'S GRACE AND STILL GROWING STRONG")

Identify the pictures and put the poster on your youth room or narthex bulletin board as a way of sharing the theme and yourselves.

Bible Study/Worship (60 min.)

Sometimes there are people we'd rather not run into. We know from past experience or just from intuition that being with them is going to be uncomfortable. Lots of times we can avoid people and situations like this. We can take another turn in the hall when we see these people coming. We can duck into a store, or we can start reading intently and giving off can't-you-see-I'm-very-busy-for-heaven's-sake-don't-bother-me signals. But sometimes there is no avoiding them. We must go through with encountering a person, intent on keeping the contact as minimal as possible.

Maybe that's what happened with the woman at the well. You can read her story in John 4:4–30. She needed water, or she probably wouldn't have come. She had no intention of talking to the man, although she had talked to plenty of men in the past. It was He, a man and obviously a Jew, who struck up the conversation. He wanted a drink of water, He said, but He had no bowl or cup. She knew (she thought) that He wouldn't drink from hers. Jews didn't use Samaritan cups. A woman and a Samaritan. She had two strikes against her. She was a black sheep if ever there was one. She said how kind He was, how warm, how willing to talk—although she didn't understand all of what He said, especially the part about the living water. "How unfair," she may have thought. "He and I could be friends if only I were a man and a Jew."

Sometimes the same thing can happen to us. We find ourselves unaccepted by others because of something that we can't help—like being a woman and a Samaritan.

Think about a time you felt unaccepted because of something that you couldn't change (and probably don't even want to change).

    Was it at home or with people your own age or with others?
    How did you feel?
    How did you react?

Have you ever found another person unacceptable because of something about him/herself that he/she couldn't change? (Or do you know of such an incident involving someone else?)

Take time to think about these questions and then share in groups of three. The woman had come only for H_2O, but the Jewish teacher spoke of living water, water that quenches thirst forever. He said He could give her that kind of water. It sounded good to her—no more daily trips to Jacob's well, burdened with jars and buckets. "Give me this water," she said. "Go call your husband," Jesus replied.

"What does He know?" she thought. "Have I seen His face before?" "I have no husband," she answered, and He agreed. "You've had five husbands, and the man you're living with now is not your husband." She was a woman with a past and a not so savory present. She had been around. She was a black sheep not only because of the fact that she was a woman and a Samaritan but because of the sinful way in which she was living. She was unacceptable not only because of the things she could not change but because of things she could do something about—like her common law marriage. Generally, folks like Jesus didn't spend time with folks like her, she probably thought. The text does not say she was shamed, but she was certainly amazed: "He told me everything I've ever done."

All of us do things of which we are ashamed. Like the lusty lady at the well, we sometimes do things we know are wrong.

Did you ever do anything that made you think or feel that your family would be ashamed of you or might not love you if they knew? that you'd lose your friends? that you couldn't love and respect yourself anymore? that God couldn't love you anymore?

Take time to think about these questions and share, if you can, in groups of three. (If you would like to share this concern with somebody, but not this group, maybe your youth counselor, pastor, or school counselor would be just the one to listen.)

Jesus not only talked to the woman who was a Samaritan and living in sin. He chose to tell her His secret. When she referred to the coming Messiah, Jesus told her: "I am He." Jesus spent a lot of time with people who had reputations much like the woman at the well. He got a lot of complaints about it too. Read Luke 15:1-7.

How does it feel to be lost? Close your eyes and give yourself a few minutes to feel alone, terrified, confused. Rely on a past experience if you can.

How does it feel to be found? Close your eyes and give yourself a few minutes to feel relieved, joyful, safe.

In Jesus' life, death, and resurrection, God is loving us with no strings attached. God's love for us does not depend on who we are nor even on our behavior. The lamb goes home cradled in the shepherd's care no matter where it has been or why.

Think of someone you love very much. Why do you love him or her? Make a list. Now go through your list and ask yourself: If this thing about the person changed, would I still love him or her?

You might notice that unlike God, who loves us no matter what (unconditional love), a lot of our human love is conditioned on what we get from the relationship. Don't let that discourage you. We're all still growing. As you grow in God's love, you will be able to love people more fully with God's unconditional love. But even then, like all humans, you will not be able to love perfectly. Still, you'll surprise yourself. Sometimes you'll find yourself caring for someone even when he or she doesn't care for you in return. Or you'll find yourself caring for someone whom it's very difficult to care for at all. Can you think of a time when that has happened already? That's God's love shining through you.

Give everyone an opportunity to thank God aloud for someone, besides God, who loves him or her very much. Sing "O Jesus, Joy of Loving Hearts" or "Love Divine, All Love Excelling" and think about the lusty lady at the well and the cradled lamb.

Recreation (20-30 min.)

Sardines is reverse Hide and Seek. "It" hides while everyone else counts to 100 together. Players then search for "it." When "it" is found, players attempt to secretively hide with "it" without giving the hiding place away to other players. This continues until everyone is crammed into one hiding place. The first one to discover "it" is the hider for the next round.

Refreshments (15–20 min.)
How about hot chocolate or spiced tea and cinnamon donuts?

Guilty
(God's Forgiveness)
by Ben Freudenburg

Objectives
To offer opportunities for participants to share their thoughts about an emotion called guilt
To learn about guilt from God's Word
To share their guilt with others
To experience God's forgiveness through confession and absolution

Materials Needed
- Bibles
- Newsprint
- Masking tape
- Newspaper
- Garbage bags
- Wash cloth
- Towels
- Buckets
- Candle

Introduction to Topic
    I was a sophomore in high school when my mother and I had a disagreement. I don't remember what I said, but it was defiant enough to deserve a slap across the face—which she immediately began to deliver. No one likes to be slapped, so I stopped the blow—until that small voice inside flooded me with the emotion called guilt. I took my hand away, and she continued with all her five-foot strength and delivered a blow that hurt my pride more than my young face.
    This youth night deals with this very emotion, guilt. Dr. James Dobson in his book *Emotions, Can You Trust Them?* defines guilt this way, "Guilt is an expression of the conscience which is a product of our emotions. It is a feeling of disapproval which is conveyed to the rational mind of what we might call the 'Department of Emotions.'" Emotions or feelings are caused by something concrete that happens to us. (Remember the feelings caused by your first date, the big lie, the birth of a child, or driving the car by yourself for the first time?)
    I believe there are two kinds of guilt: healthy guilt, a feeling that comes when we are caught doing wrong, and unhealthy guilt, a feeling that manipulates us even though we have done no wrong. There was a time I felt guilty when I quit the basketball team because my family wanted me home during Thanksgiving and Christmas. I felt guilty not being with them even though I had done nothing wrong. It's this unhealthy guilt that Satan uses to plague and drive us away from Christ.
    As we share guilt, we need to be aware of two things. First, guilt is a feeling caused by failure. It is difficult to share failure because no one likes to condemn oneself. Therefore, the leader has to be willing to share his or her failures in a real way if he or she expects others to do so. Second, as one is sharing, he or she needs to recognize the difference between healthy and unhealthy guilt. Healthy guilt is a feeling caused by the recognition that we have sinned against God. Unhealthy guilt only needs to be recognized for what it is. I pray this resource might help the young people you serve. May they share about the sin that causes the guilt—and then share in the fantastic

feeling of joy that comes from the healing power of our Father's forgiveness through Jesus Christ.

Emotional Bop

This game is played with everyone sitting in a circle. Each person substitutes an emotion for his or her name (avoid duplications). Go around the circle a few times to get acquainted with each other's "new identity." Choose a person to be "it." "It" is armed with a pillow and stands in the middle of the circle. (Make sure all youth and adults and especially the leader play.)

To start, the leader calls out an emotion like "hate." "It" tries to hit "hate" with the pillow before "hate" can call out another emotion like "joy." The round continues until "it" can bop an emotion before another emotion is called. Play the game for about 10 minutes. (*Note:* If your group is new or there are several guests, play the game first with real names and then rename with emotions.)

A Word About Emotions

Read or restate in your own words the following: Feelings are caused by something real that has happened in our lives. (It is very important for the leader to share a personal feeling experienced in his or her life as an example. Share deeply, openly, and honestly.)

Name That Feeling

This is an exercise that will help us practice sharing our feelings. The leader reads the sentence and lets the people share the feeling it produced in them.

1. I got the highest grade in the class on the test. Name that feeling.
2. I just flunked my driving test. Name that feeling.
3. Mom just told us she's pregnant. Name that feeling.
4. *Boys only:* My girlfriend just told me that she's pregnant. Name that feeling.
5. *Girls only:* The man of my dreams just asked me out. Name that feeling.
6. *Boys only:* She accepted. Name that feeling.
7. I just told a lie and got away with it. Name that feeling.
8. I bought my first car. Name that feeling.
9. I cheated on a test. Name that feeling.
10. I screamed at my parents. Name that feeling.

After doing the preceding exercise, share the following: Guilt is a feeling that is produced when we are caught doing wrong. (Add some of your own thoughts about guilt, but keep them short and to the point. Think about these questions. What role does the conscience play in guilt, and where does the guilt come from? What's the difference between healthy and unhealthy guilt?)

Bible Study (10 min.)

If your group has 10 to 12 people, do the study together. If it's larger, break into smaller groups to read one of the stories below, answer the questions, and report back to the others. It's best if participants record their answers on newsprint and show them as a report.

> **Prodigal Son** (Luke 15:11–24)
> **David and Bathsheba** (2 Sam. 11–12:25)
> Who felt the guilt?
> What was the sin? What caused the guilt?
> Was it healthy guilt? Why?
> How do you suppose the guilt was good for David?

A Game with Newspaper

This game is to help the participants deductively discover what guilt is and how Jesus takes the sin and guilt away. You will need

> a court marked with masking tape that provides about one square yard per person on a team with a dividing line across the center;
> a large stack of newspaper for each team;
> a number of garbage bags;
> one wash cloth and towel for every two people; and

a number of buckets filled with warm sudsy water.

Mark the court; divide the group into two teams; and place the newspaper in each court.

Round 1

Give these directions: I will give you a topic, and you are to find a news report. The group that brings the article to me first gets a point. (Give the winning group a prize. Candy bars work great!) Here are some topics:

A murder	Traffic violation
Robbery	Traffic fatality
A rape	Dirty movie advertisement
Child abuse	

Round 2

Just for fun see which group can build the highest tower of newspaper. Be sure to bring a tape measure and have a ladder handy. You might want to set some rules. If you have a large group, with over 30 on a side, see which group can hide the most people in the newspaper in a given time period.

Round 3

The winner of the paper war is the side that has the least amount of paper in its court at the end of three one-minute rounds.

Rules: You may not cross the center line or leave your court.

All paper outside the court does not count.

Round 4

The winner is the group that can stuff the paper in the least number of garbage bags.

Rules: Divide all the paper into equal piles in the two courts.

Have the plastic bags available and say "go."

Discussion

Have all the participants get in a circle with their knees touching. Ask them this question: "If newspaper represents the sin in our lives, what could the black all over your hands symbolize?" When guilt comes up, you might say, "Yes, just like this yucky black ink is all over us, sin leaves us with a yucky feeling called guilt. Wouldn't it feel great to get this black stuff off us?"

Divide into pairs and hand out the towels, wash cloths, and soapy water. Have the pairs decide who is A and who is B. Then ask A to wash the black off B and vice versa.

After all are clean, get back into one circle and say you have a riddle that needs an answer. "If the newspaper is a symbol for sin and the black is a symbol for the feeling of guilt, what's the water? the soap? the wash cloth?" Then read Eph. 1:7. Ask how the passage ties into what you have done and discussed.

Share—It's Worth the Risk

In your group of 12 to 15 ask each member to share the first time he or she remembers being spanked or disciplined as a child. The leader should also share his or her account, being sure to be honest. Go around the circle, allowing individuals the freedom to pass. Assure tham that it's okay not to share. Next tell them that as children they probably didn't feel guilt that sharply, but as they moved into junior high, things probably began to bother them. Ask group members to list four to six actions of teenagers that, in their opinion, most causes the feeling of guilt. Write them on the chalkboard or newsprint.

Next, you as leader share the item that caused you the most guilt in high school. Ask if others would like to share something that frequently causes them to feel guilty.

Ask the youth what they do with their guilt. Do they (a) face it and ask for relief? (b) run? (c) try to forget it? or (d) rationalize it away? Does guilt make us feel inferior or inadequate? Why? What can we do about it?

Confession—Absolution

Place a candle in the middle of the room and stand around it with arms around one another's shoulders. Turn off the lights.

Open with a song: "Father, I Adore You," "Spirit of the Living God," or "Kum-Ba-Ya."

Then say, "Tonight we've shared our failures and how these failures produce guilt in us. We've also shared how Jesus washes our sin and guilt away through His death. As a closing tonight we will be offered the opportunity to confess out loud our sins. To confess your sins, just say: 'Father, forgive me for . . .,' and finish the sentence with the sin you wish to confess. The rest of us will respond by saying: 'You are forgiven; feel guilty no more!' "

The leader must start and confess a real sin in his or her life. Your honesty will encourage others to also be honest.

After those who wish have confessed their sin, give a corporate absolution like: "Because Christ has died for payment for your sin, you are forgiven and free from the guilt of sin. In the name of the Father, Son, and Holy Spirit. Amen."

Afterglow

No food, just Christian hugs.

Option

If the above Confession-Absolution is too heavy for your group, remember: sins can be burned away if written on paper, exploded away by a cross with a straight pin taped to it if written on balloons with permanent magic markers, or washed off if written on a plastic overhead sheet.

Remember the Able/Disabled

by Sharon Schuh and Kay Stoll

I asked Jesus, "How much do You love me?"

Jesus said, "This much . . ."

and He stretched out His arms and died.

Objectives

To become aware that we all possess certain disabilities
To express care for the disabled
To learn to bring people to wholeness and healing through the sharing of the Gospel

Materials Needed

    Role cards
    Bibles
    Newsprint
    Materials for roleplay i.e., wheelchairs, eye patches, paper tape or string, alphabet board
    Construction paper

Introduction to Topic

Many physical disabilities are obvious; their effect on the person with the disability is not so obvious. Many people with handicaps feel rejected, alienated, and useless. But those feelings are not unique to the disabled. Even so-called "normal" young people sometimes feel unlovely or unloved, talentless, resourceless, powerless, or alone. Everyone, disabled or not, wants to be more accepted by others—especially by the others in the body of Christ. Young people tend to focus so much of their attention on their own inner hurts and fears that they often seem callous to others who suffer more severe physical and emotional disabilities. Through their learning experiences we want to help participants learn to reach out more effectively to the disabled by experiencing, if only briefly and inadequately, what it means to have a serious disability.

Preparation

This evening's experience can be done in a variety of ways. You will want to choose procedures to fit the needs of your youth group. You might want to ask a person in your congregation with a physical disability to help you design this learning experience or refer to the films and books listed.

One good way for able-bodied people to experience a disability is through simulation. A chance to roleplay a disability and its effects can help young people appreciate the effects of permanent disabilities. You might want to enhance your simulation roleplay by gathering materials and borrowing equipment from hospitals, nursing homes, or hospital supply outlets. For example, provide a few wheelchairs for those who will play the parts of the quadra or paraplegic; blindfolds or eye patches to simulate visual handicaps; and paper tape, string, or belts to tie limbs and fingers of those who will be partially paralyzed. Those who will simulate the inability to speak should use an alphabet board to communicate. (To make an alphabet board, paste letters on cardboard. Speech-impaired people use this board to speak by pointing to the letters of the words they want to say.) With this equipment, create as many disabled roles as you desire. On individual cards write out disabilities to be roleplayed and the equipment required for each disability. For instance: "Mary has paralyzed legs and uses a wheelchair." "John has poor muscle coordination and a speech problem. He uses a cane to walk and an alphabet board to speak." One card will be given to each participant.

Icebreaker (10 min.)

List or draw some parts of the body on the board or newsprint. You might include a mouth, an eye, a brain, a stomach, a foot, a hand, a nose. Encourage each participant to select the part of the body he or she feels most like—at least on this particular evening. Let the participants in turn tell their names and why they chose a particular part of the body. If you have time, you might let participants draw the part of the body they have identified with on construction paper. Let them print their names on their creations, cut them out, and wear them as "name tags."

Bible Study "One Body with Many Parts" (15–30 min.)

Read 1 Cor. 12:12–16 aloud.

Use the following discussion questions to help youth identify how their bodies are both able and disabled at the same time.

1. What parts of yourself do you see as disabled or imperfect? Are you too tall, too short, too shy, or too poor in grades or sports? Do you have hay fever, too many freckles, or a big nose?
2. What parts of yourself are good and "able"? Do you have a friendly smile, a sense of humor, scholastic ability, or an ability to understand others? Do you read, bake, organize or dress well?

Let participants share some of their responses to both questions in groups of 3 to 4.

Read Eph. 4:15–16 aloud.

Without Jesus we are disjointed. Under Christ's control we fit and are held together. Discuss: With Christ as our Head, how can we do more understanding of each other's abilities and disabilities?

Simulation, Recreation, and Afterglow (75 min.)

Spend as much time as you can in your simulation roles. Your usual time for recreation and refreshment are also included in the simulation exercise. Let each participant select a "disabled" role card and locate the equipment needed to simulate that disability. After a time, refreshments can be served. Encourage some of the less "disabled" to assist others in eating, drinking, and carrying food. Note the cooperation needed in your discussion about how the various parts of the body function together. For recreation, post a list of specific activities. Each person is to attempt all of these, though it might be well to keep inexperienced wheelchair operators away from steps.

Activities

1. Go to the altar with communion in mind.
2. Use the restrooms. Use the mirror in the restroom.
3. Make a phone call.
4. Get a drink of water.
5. Clean up and throw away garbage.
6. Take dishes to the kitchen.

Many other activities can be designed depending on your church accommodations. Be sure to encourage participants to identify and remember their feelings as they attempt each task.

Discussion

When the simulation is over, move participants into groups of four and let them discuss the following questions: How did you feel as you "lived with a disability?" What was particularly difficult? How did others help or hinder you?

Ask groups to share some of their discussion with the whole group.

Reflect

Brainstorm and make a list (put it on the chalkboard or newsprint) of things I (we) have done (left undone) that have made it harder for persons with disabilities to be a part of the body of Christ here.

Let small groups discuss your list. Encourage them to include a time of repentance in their discussion. After about 10 minutes, as they report on their sharing, be sure to speak the Good News of God's forgiveness in Jesus Christ.

Act

Brainstorm again and make another list of things we can do to make people with disabilities more fully a part of the body of Christ here. Be sure to make plans to act on some of the participants' suggestions.

Worship

Scripture

Rom. 12:1

Opening Song

"Take My Life, O Lord, Renew"

Gospel Message

John 15:1–5

Responsive Prayer

Lord, create in us a spirit of thankfulness for Your love for us and increase our love for one another. We repent of our past resentment of our own disabilities and our rejection of others who have disabilities. Forgive us. Help us to grow from our own disabilities and to reach out in love to others—especially others who are disabled. Show us how to love each person with the same kind of love that You have for us. We ask this in Your precious name. Amen.

Closing Song

"Abide with Me," stanza 1

Resources

Films

Rental $25–$35, 16mm, color
> *Handicapism* (20 min.), *It's a New Day* (9 min.), *A Different Approach* (21 min.)
>> Available from: CENTS
>> 731 21st Ave. South
>> Minneapolis, MN 55454
>> Telephone: (612) 330-1140
>
> *A Day in the Life of Bonnie Consolo* (28 min)
>> Available from: Concordia Film Service
>> 3558 South Jefferson Avenue
>> St. Louis, MO 63118
>> Telephone: 1-800-325-3040

Other sources for films are public and college libraries, organizations for the disabled, and vocational rehabilitation centers.

Reading Resources

One Body—One Mission: Suggestions for Christian Ministries with Disabled Persons in the Local Congregation. Copyright 1981 Augsburg Publishing House, Concordia Publishing House, and Fortress Press.

On Hidden Talents: A Study of Physical Disabilities in Relation to God's Plan in Christ. Copyright 1981 Augsburg Publishing House and Concordia Publishing House.

Ministry with the Handicapped packet. Joyce Peltzer. American Lutheran Church, 422 S. 5th Street, Minneapolis, MN 55415.

Ear Wax and Cotton
(Being Better Listeners)

by Steve Rice

Objectives

To become aware of and repent of what interferes with listening to God and others
To learn how to actively listen to God and others
To develop new ways to serve others who have hurts and joys by being better listeners

Materials Needed

> Poster picture of ear
> Encyclopedia
> Bible
> Chalkboard or newsprint
> Q-Tips

Pre-Evening Preparation

You may want to use a poster of the ear or other publicity materials as a symbol for this experience. The first few words of Is. 55:3 might serve as an appropriate invitation, "Incline (bend) your ear (listen) and *come to ME!*" says the Lord to each of us.

A large poster picture of an ear might serve as a name board. As participants arrive, each person puts his or her name on some part of the ear. Resource materials (such as an encyclopedia) might help participants discover the function of their chosen parts. Or you might assign someone to research the parts and function of their chosen parts or of the human ear. Those who are not sure of the function of a particular ear part could ask the resource person.

Icebreakers (10 min.)

1. Silent Introduction. Without talking or using words (drawing and pantomine are okay) each is to discover the following about another:
   a. Place of birth (state or province)
   b. Favorite TV show
   c. Favorite ice cream
   d. One hope for the future

   Bring the group together and ask several individuals to introduce themselves or each other from the information they were able to pick up.
2. Loudest Introduction. See who can introduce himself or herself the loudest. The leader may want to have participants do this all at the same time. Provide cotton to protect the ears and limit the activity to just a couple of minutes.
3. Decorate the Ear. Divide the group into equal teams of five or less. Have each group decorate an ear. The ear can belong to a member of the group or be a version the members draw on paper. The decorations can be costume jewelry, paper and yarn, whipping cream, or whatever.

   Vote on the most attractive ear.

Recreation (20 min.)

1. Sculpturing Contest: Let each person or small group sculpture an ear out of clay, ice, snow, whipping cream, or whatever can be molded. Give recognition to the best one.
2. Ear Beauty Contest: Ask for several volunteers to be part of the Beautiful Ear Contest. Select others to be judges. The judges should decide on what basis they will judge the contestants' ears. Some contestants may have the ability to "wiggle" their ears as the talent part of the contest. Let judges select the most beautiful ear, the most unusual, etc.
3. Name That Hymn. This game is similar to "Name That Tune." Invite an organist or pianist to help you with this game or tape the hymns you want to use. Divide the group into four teams or less. Each team member is to challenge an opposing member to guess the tune of a familiar church hymn or song in as few notes as possible. Points can be awarded to the team whose member guesses the tune correctly. Based on total points, a team is declared the winner and moves on to challenge another team.
4. Select other games (check your local library or church library for game books) that require participants to listen to directions or challenges their ability to listen.

Learning Experience

The Bible stresses the importance of the gift of hearing and our need to improve our ability to listen and hear. For instance, Jesus' example as He healed (see Mark 5:30–33, for example) and taught (Luke 24:13–25) indicate how important He thought listening was as He ministered to those in need. And James, as He recounts some of the features of our discipleship, indicates that we are to be "quick to hear" (James 1:19).

Introduction: A Demonstration of Listening

Have a stereo unit available with either a stereo tape or a stereo test record. As the group gathers around, demonstrate the stereo channels by switching the balance control from one speaker to the other. Note how difficult it is to pick out the channels when the balance is equal. Turn the volume up high and down so low that it can't be heard. Note how the differences affect our listening. Indicate to group members that there are four steps they will take as they develop their listening ability.

Step 1: Why Can't I Hear? (10 min.)

Purpose: That the participants may be able to identify the *ear wax* (original sin) and *cotton* (actual sin) stuck in their ears.

Procedure: Brainstorm and list (on a chalkboard or on newsprint) the reasons we don't always hear others' cries and calls for help. Then list reasons we don't really hear what is said by others. Reasons might include the following: I'm thinking while the other is speaking, outside noise, poor hearing, the other person speaks too softly, etc. Reasons for not hearing are many. Some of them are due to *wax* (our sinful nature interfering), and some are due to *cotton* (when we choose not to hear). Explain the two categories, write them on the board, and try to put the reason for our failure to hear in the proper categories. Take some time for repentance (silently or shared) as you consider these failures and faults.

Step 2: How Do I Get My Ears to Hear What God and Others Are Saying to Me? (20 min.)

Purpose: That participants may develop a method of learning how to listen actively.

Definition of *Active Listening:* Reflecting to the message sender or speaker my understanding of what he or she is communicating without judging the content of the message. You may want to put this definition (or one like it) on the chalkboard or on newsprint. Discuss the statement and refine it as a group so that you are sure everyone understands the definitions.

Procedure: Write the following on a piece of newsprint (or a chalkboard that can be left unerased for the evening):

Surface Feeling:	I feel MAD	I feel SAD	I feel GLAD	I feel AFRAID
waves	~~~~~	~~~~~	~~~~~	~~~~~
Undercurrent:	what HURTS?	what HURTS?	what is GOOD?	what is the potential HURT?
Inner Result:	what I've LOST	what I've LOST	what I've GAINED	What I might POSSIBLY LOSE

Label this whole design a "Feeling Flow Chart" and explain that you are going to give three examples to help participants understand the chart. Ask participants to put themselves in the place of the speaker in each example and to try to identify the speaker's feelings.

EXAMPLE No. 1: "My class just elected me secretary of the class!"

Discuss: What *surface feeling* can you identify in this speaker? (I feel glad.) What *lies behind* that surface happiness? (I am successful, well liked, and accepted.) What is the *inner result?* (I've gained assurance, pride, and confidence.)

EXAMPLE No. 2: "No one even nominated me for any of the class offices."

Discuss: What is the *surface feeling?* (probably mad or sad—note how similar these feelings are) What is the *undercurrent?* (hurt or loneliness or rejection) What is the *inner result?* (loss of pride or self-esteem)

EXAMPLE No. 3: "I just found out my parents are getting a divorce, and it's all my mom's fault."

Discuss: What are the *surface feelings?* (probably sad at first, then angry) What is the *undercurrent?* (I'm going to get hurt.) What is the *inner result?* (My life and relationships are coming apart.)

Review the definition of *active listening.* Our unplugged ears listen for the *surface feelings* and what lies behind those feelings. As we listen to feelings as well as words, we begin to understand what the speaker is really saying about himself or herself.

Step 3: Listening with Unstopped Ears (20 min.)

Purpose: That participants may practice listening for feelings.
Procedure: Participants should work in pairs on the next three experiences.

Experience A: Ask participants to fill in the blank and answer the questions, then share their responses with their partners. Write the following statement and questions on the board (newsprint) for participants to copy.
Statement: "When my teacher told me to be quiet in class, it really _____ _____."
What is your *surface feeling* in this situation?
What is the *undercurrent*—the hidden message?
What is the *inner result*? (What is lost?)

Experience B: Ask one of the partners to read Ps. 54. Pairs should discuss the following questions, focusing particularly on verses 6 and 7.
What was David's *surface feeling*?
What lay *under his feeling*?
What was the *inner result* for him?

Experience C: Ask the other partner to read John 14:8–21. Pairs should discuss the same set of questions as they relate to Jesus.

Step 4: Sharing What You Have Heard (15 min.)

Purpose: That the participants may focus on and share their discoveries as they practice active listening.

Procedure: Let pairs share some of their experiences. Encourage volunteers to summarize what listening for feelings is all about. Note some of these definitions on the board.

As time permits, suggest that individuals share a personal experience with a partner. The pairs can then seek to understand the experience by comparing it to the *Feeling Flow Chart*. Then let participants share with another partner a particularly good or bad experience. The listener is to identify feelings and reflect them back to the speaker (you are hurt, angry, happy, etc.). Reverse the roles and repeat.

Worship Experience (15 min.)

The purpose of this worship experience is to give participants the opportunity to report on their past failure to hear, to receive forgiveness for this, and to rededicate themselves to a ministry of listening. Choose an opening hymn that reflects the fact that we come to God in worship just as we are, with wax-filled and cotton-stuffed ears. Two possibilities are "Just as I Am" or "They Hung Him on a Tree."

After the hymn, allow four to six minutes for *silent* reflection. Let the psalm of praise come from the group. Each should repeat the phrase and add an appropriate word. Psalm of Praise: "O Lord, I praise and thank You for _____" (indicate the noise that was heard).

Use a collect like this: We thank you, O God, for our ears and the sounds that fill them—for the sound of the seas and the rain, of horns and flutes, of basketballs and voices. Help us to listen more closely to the hurts and pain, the joys and fears, the cries and calls that are all around us. Help us to communicate our care as we share and let others know that we understand. In Jesus' name. Amen.

Confession: Hand out a slip of paper to each person. Individuals should note the *ear wax* and *cotton* that get in the way of their listening to those around them.

Absolution: Hand out a Q-Tip to each person as you collect the confession. These Q-Tips stand for the Communication Tips you have received. God communicated His grace to us as He forgives our sins (wax and cotton) because of Jesus Christ.

Read John 15:13–15. Let participants discuss what Jesus is saying to them. What do they *hear* in the words of the Savior? Sing a song of thanksgiving as a reponse.

For your closing prayer let each person speak about something for which he or she feels grateful.

Close with the benediction. As a sign of blessing, each person may touch another's ears and say, "May the Lord bless you and use your hearing to His glory."

Afterglow (15-20 min.)

Cooked ears of corn (if available) might make an appropriate snack. Cookies made in the shape of ears might serve to jog some informal discussion.

Money Is Power?

by Steve Sonnenberg

Objectives

To look at the value young people put on money
To discover the correlation between money and power

Materials Needed

    Bibles
    Paper
    Pencils
    15 cups of grain (such as unpopped popcorn)
    1,200 pennies (Have youth bring these from home.)
    8 plastic measuring cups with gradations from 1/8 to 1 cup
    One index card (or piece of paper) with a penny stuck to it for each person
    7 index cards (3" x 5") for game (Write "Good Luck" on 3 cards, "Bad Luck" on 2, and "Great Luck" on 2.)
    Tape or pin
    Offering plate
    Several pairs of mittens (the bulkier the better)

Getting Acquainted (15 min.)

Give youth a blank sheet of paper and pencil as they arrive. Fold the paper in half lengthwise and number from 1 to 15 down the left side. Ask them to pretend that they have each just received $1,000. The only condition is that they must spend the total amount on 10 to 15 different things. They are to list the items they would purchase or the causes to which they would donate (and the amount spent on each) on the left side of their papers—one item per number. The total of all items cannot exceed $1,000. When several people have finished, they should circulate and compare lists. Allow latecomers to complete their lists before they join in. Have youth write the names of others beside the items that appear on both of their lists. Allow enough time for everyone to look at everyone's list. If your group is too large, stop after 20 minutes in order to begin the discussion.

Discussion (20 min.)

Have the participants form groups of fours and discuss these quesitons:
1. What did you discover about how you would use money?
2. Notice how many names of other people you have written beside each of the items you listed. What does this tell you about how you are like or unlike the other people at this meeting?
3. If you had only $100 to spend (instead of $1,000), which items would you choose? Why?
4. If you had it to do over, which items would you take off your list? What items would you add?

Bring everyone together in a large group and conclude this discussion with the question: How important is money and the way you would use it?

Money Is Power Game (75 min.)

(Adapted from "Real World Game," *Ideas*, Vol. 13C, 1974, Youth Specialties, 1224 Greenfield Dr., El Cajon, CA 92021. Used by permission.)

The following is a simulation game designed to allow your youth group to experience how much power comes from having access to money. Whether it is a country, a school district, a family, or a youth, the one with money has power. The game involves seven teams of one or more persons. Teams do not have to be equal sizes. If your group has fewer than seven persons, arbitrarily select any number of teams. The number of teams will not significantly affect the outcome of the game.

Materials needed for this activity have been listed at the beginning of this article. Although most of the instructions are included on the Money is Power fact sheet, the leader needs to do these things:

1. Have all the supplies measured and ready for distribution before the games begins.
2. Remember to take the monthly consumptions and give of monthly production and income between each time period.
3. Between each time period collect the "Luck" cards, reshuffle them, and have each team draw one. This should be done before a new period begins.
4. Refrain from giving additional instructions or answering questions once the game is in process.

If your situation calls for a different number of teams than seven, then you will need to make a new fact sheet. In setting up a different situation, make sure the total production of all teams is slightly more than the total needed. This will allow (at least theoretically) survival of all teams.

Money Is Power Fact Sheet

Team	Direct Trading Teams	Per period Production	Per period Needs	Per period Income
1	All items	2 cups	1/2 cup	$ .30
2	1,3,5, only	1 1/2 cups	3 cups	.10
3	All but 6	1/2 cup	2/3 cup	.30
4	All but 2	3/4 cup	2 cups	.10
5	All but 6	1/4 cup	1 cup	.40
6	1,4,7 only	2 1/2 cups	1 1/2 cups	.20
7	All but 2	2 1/2 cups	1 1/4 cups	.50

If you are not allowed to trade with teams directly, it may be done through a neutral team acting as an intermediary. A neutral team is one that can trade directly with the teams that want to negotiate.

Game Directions

Goal: Your purpose is to survive as a team and acquire as much wealth as possible in whatever way you choose—beg, borrow, buy, (or steal!).

Getting ready: Form teams by counting off by sevens. Give each team a name tag with its team number on it (1 to 7). The Ambassador should wear the team number. Teams should gather in different parts of the room to select their leaders and study the fact sheet. If teams are large enough, the following officers should be chosen:

Team Leader

Leads in deciding his/her team's policies and negotiates with other teams who come to his/her team.

Ambassador

Negotiates for the team with other teams. You may select more than one ambassador if you feel the need.

Treasurer

Keeps, oversees, and guards the money and grain.

Game Rules
1. The game is played in time periods. There will be six periods of eight minutes each. At the beginning of each period, you will receive your monthly income and grain quotas. At the end of each period, you will have your period consumption taken away (grain needs). In the eight minutes alloted, your job is to accumulate or maintain enough grain to survive the period. It is also possible to build up your grain possessions for cash refund at the end of the game. Remember, too, the Christian concerns of caring and sharing.
2. When time is called at the end of each period, all negotiations must stop.
3. At the beginning of each period, except the first, each team leader will draw a "luck" card. The cards will say "Good Luck," "Bad Luck," or "Great Luck." "Good Luck" means no change in grain allotment. "Bad Luck" means that your grain allotment will be increased by 1 cup if your usual allotment is large or by 1/2 cup if your usual allotment is small. Begin the next period as soon as all allotments have been made and the teams have had five minutes to discuss their philosophy. Continue until six periods have been completed. At the end of round six, take away the period consumption of grain and redeem any leftover grain from teams at the rate of .02 per 1/4 cup.
4. Catastrophe. If your team does not have enough grain at the end of any time period to fulfill its "take away or need" quota, it meets with catastrophe and is out of the game.

Conclusion

Discuss with youth
1. how they felt during the game;
b. what difference varying allotments of money made;
c. in what way money and power are connected; and
d. what was learned in this game.

Closing Worship (15 min.)

Read 1 Tim. 6:6–10, 17–19

Point out the specifics of Paul's concerns for wealth and the use of it. You could ask the youth to identify the pitfalls of too much money and too much power. Focus on how money and power can be used for the benefit of Christ's kingdom. Remember to refer to actual experiences discovered during the listing and sharing of how each person would have spent his/her $1,000 as well as during the Money Is Power game. Distribute index cards (with a penny glued to the upper left-hand corner) and pencils to everyone. These cards are "A Penny for Your Thoughts" prayers. Each person should write a prayer on the card. The prayer topics should center on money, its power, and especially its influence in the life of the writer.

Collect the cards in an offering plate. Conclude the worship by reading the prayers and asking God's blessing on how the people in your group make and spend their money.

Recreation and Refreshments (25 min.)

The purpose of these suggested activities is to deemphasize the significance of money—to have fun, to play. Several suggestions follow. Select any of those which fit.

You will need lots of pennies for these games. The more the merrier. You can use the pennies used in the Money Is Power game. Have the young people bring some from home or provide them yourself.

Pick-a-Pocket

Divide the pennies equally. The object is to put as many pennies as possible in the pockets of other people. Take care not to tear pockets. There are two variations of the game:

Option A—you cannot take pennies out of your pocket. The person with the most pennies in his or her pocket after 10 minutes is the loser.

Option B—you can take money out of your pocket to put in someone else's pocket. The same 10-minute time period applies. Play two or more rounds. If money is dropped, the person dropping it must pick it up.

Penny Relay

Divide into teams of six to eight persons. Line up in single file. Give each team a penny. Each person must race one at a time to the end of the room while balancing the penny on his or her nose. No hands! If the money falls off, it must be picked up and returned to the nose, and the runner must resume the race at the place he or she was when the money fell. Number one races to the end of the room, returns to line, and hands the penny to the next person in line before that person races to the end of the room and back. (Continue in typical relay fashion.)

Penny Sculpture

Divide into teams of four to six persons. Give each team an equal amount of pennies. Have them build a sculpture with their money.

Penny Pick-up

Have several pairs of mittens and lots of pennies lying flat on a table. Take turns giving each person an opportunity to pick up as many pennies as possible in one minute while wearing a pair of mittens. (No fair pushing money to or off the edge of the table.)

Penny Power

Distribute money equally to everyone. Allow five minutes for people to give away their money to each other. The only rule is that you cannot give more than three pennies to any one person at any one time. At the end of the game the people who have the fewest pennies win. The others should take their money home or contribute to some project. (Don't tell participants about keeping the money until after the game ends.)

Refreshments

Pop the corn used in the Money Is Power game and serve fruit juice. Bake cupcakes. Wash and wrap some money and drop it in some of the cupcakes before baking them. Warn people to watch out because there are surprises in some of the cupcakes.

I Am My Job

by Margaret Rickers

Objectives

To become aware that we are more than our jobs
To explore expectations for a job, as well as the expectations of a future employer
To examine vocations and special qualifications for these choices

Materials Needed

>Paper
>Pencils
>Newsprint
>Masking tape
>Body-part cards

Icebreaker: Who Am I? (25–30 min.)

As the group gathers, share tonight's topic about jobs. Have youth choose an occupation that provides alliteration with their names, like Busboy Brian, Seamstress Susan, Nurse Nancy, or Singer

Steve. Have the youth go around the circle and introduce themselves with these titles. Use the names throughout the evening.

(Following are two alternate icebreakers.)

Alternate 1

(This exercise can be used with "What's My Line?" at the end of this topic.)

It is important for youth to think of their positive traits, which make them more than their jobs. To encourage their thoughts, use the following exercise: Provide each with a large piece of paper preferably 8 1/2 x 14 inches). Have youth write their first names in large letters vertically down the side of the paper.

Then have them use the letters in their name to start different adjectives that describe themselves. The adjectives should reflect something about themselves—either positive or negative. This is called an acrostic.

For example:

Ambitious	Jovial
Nervous	Outgoing
Neat	Excited

Encourage the youth to share the alliterations they made with their names and the acrostic that was made from their first names. Help them see this as a positive experience which they are able to share with their peers.

Alternate 2

(Use this when playing the team game instead of "What's My Line?".)

In advance write single occupations on slips of paper. Choose traditional and nontraditional occupations, for instance, computer programmer, doctor, teacher, sanitation engineer, astronaut, etc. Have one slip for each group member.

Ask each person to write a job description for that occupation giving clues to the job, but not telling anyone what it actually is. Information such as educational requirements, personality traits, hours, and appropriate dress should be included. Give the youth about 10 minutes to write these in classified-ad style.

When everyone has written a brief description (25–40 words) on a paper, have the youth hand in the papers, shuffle them, and then pass out the papers again. Take turns around the circle reading the job descriptions and having the youth guess what job is described in the information. (Don't forget to use people's occupational names as suggested in 1 above.)

Where Are You Going?

1. Read the following parable to the group:
   Once there was a college graduate who didn't have a job. He made inquiries in grocery stores, restaurants, and clothing stores, but they wanted people with experience. Since he was a computer science major, he went to apply for a job at a computer store. He was sure he could get a job there—after all, he had experience in that field. The store even had a sign in the window that read: "NOW HIRING." He was ecstatic. As he walked in, he came face-to-face with a computer. The instructions on the screen said. "Please respond to the questions as appropriate. Type in the word 'Begin' when you are ready." The brilliant computer science major did as he was instructed. The first question the computer asked was, "What qualifications do you have to work here?" He promptly listed his degrees, his schools, and his grade-point average in college. The computer spit back another question, "Anything else?" The computer science major was puzzled for a few minutes and then decided it was a trick question, so he replied, "What else could you possibly require?" The computer answered, "I was hoping you would say you liked computers and other people who work with computers too! Sorry, you're not the person for our job!"
2. Ask the youth what they see as a moral to this parable. Try to draw out the fact that simply having a title, degrees, and high grades won't necessarily get the job you desire. The qualifications for a job do include these things, but one must know his or her gifts and personality well in order to apply. It is also important to know what the employer expects

from the employee before entering into a work relationship. After all, being successful in a job is more than just doing the tasks!

3. Using a large piece of newsprint, have the youth brainstorm about their expectations for a positive job situation. Consideration should be given to hours, travel, salary, benefits, education, and working relationships with other people. Encourage the youth to be as specific as possible. Then try as a group to get concensus on what item is first priority, which is second, and so on. (This may be difficult—you may have some youth argue strongly in order to win agreement. Majority wins!)

4. As important as it is to know what to look for in a job, an individual also has to recognize personal gifts that meet the expectations of an employer. This might be a sensitive issue since youth are often hesitant to brag about gifts they have for such a situation. Emphasize that these gifts are from God by reading aloud Rom. 11:33–36. Have the youth write down at least three God-given gifts that might be useful to them in an occupation. If the tone of the evening allows, have them share one or two of these gifts with the group. If you deem it inappropriate, have them spend a few minutes in silent reflection on how they might use these gifts.

5. Reference might also be made to the creation account in Gen. 1 and 2, emphasizing that we were created in God's image for a specific purpose on earth. You will need to reinforce positive traits in individuals who might feel they are insignificant. Read the creation account in Gen. 1:26–31 with this emphasis in mind.

6. Finally, as a closing to this part of the evening, have the youth write personal resumés for jobs they would like. While writing their resumés, youth should be reminded that, although a meaningful occupation is important, there is more to life than just having a job. Have them use a form that includes these items:

    Personal Biographical Information: (name, birthday, address, phone)
    Educational Background: (schools attended, what years, degree attained)
    Personality Characteristics: (works well with people, moody, easy-going, organized)
    Aspirations: (goals for job, family, etc.)
    Outside Commitments: (family, church, community involvement)
    Other Pertinent Data:

7. In groups of two or three, have the youth share their job resumés. Compare characteristics and discuss within the group whether individuals have adequately described themselves in their resumés. Discuss the following questions:
    a. Am I the type of person who can be consumed with a job and not take time for myself?
    b. What kind of job would I best be suited for?
    c. How can I guard against my job becoming master of my life?
    d. Share any interesting insights, comments, or questions for a few minutes in a large group.

Worship

Begin the worship with the song "Worship the Lord" (see *Resources for Youth Ministry*, 82.3). Then tell the group that it is important to realize that we all have different gifts to use in our occupations.

Conclude with the following exercise to emphasize this point:

1. Use masking tape for a large (six feet long if possible) stick person on the floor. (The masking tape can be placed on almost any surface without causing damage, and the youth can walk on the tape during the evening if necessary).

2. You also will need to prepare pieces of paper (equal to the number of students present) with names of different parts of the body, such as hands, heart, mouth, and so on. Try to include most of the major body parts, such as limbs and head. If the group is large, you can add toes, fingers, ears, etc.

3. Youth will draw a card from the pile and go to the place on the stick figure represented by the card. Youth should be instructed to link arms as you give a Bible to the person with the card marked "mouth." The "mouth" should read aloud 1 Cor. 12:14–31. Close with a prayer for the group as active members of the body of Christ with different gifts and functions.

Reaction

1. "What's My Line?" (to be used with alternate 1 icebreaker). This is a take-off on the old television show. Prepare slips of paper with several different bizarre occupations on them (hang glider in the mountains of Colorado, window washer in the Sears Tower in Chicago) from which the "contestants" can draw. Have the first "contestant" draw an occupation and prepare for questions by two panels of youth who will ask one question at a time that can be answered by yes or no. Go around the room in 20-questions style until the occupation is guessed by some member of the panel.
2. Team Game (to be used with alternate 2 in the icebreaker). Since we have had a fairly intense evening, play a light-hearted team game like touch football or softball. Emphasize the importance of everyone's position or "job" on the team.

Refreshments

Make your own pizza by assigning everyone a different "job"; one person can be a tomato sauce spreader; another, the olive placer; someone else, the sausage slicer, etc.

Bare Branches—A Chance to Cry
(Sharing Struggles and Hurts)

by Joani Lillevold Schultz

Objectives

To provide a time for sharing struggles, hurts, and deep concerns
To give participants the privilege of ministering to each other

Materials Needed

    A leafless branch anchored in a pot or Christmas tree stand
    Blue construction paper
    String or yarn
    Hymnals
    Bibles for everyone
    Tape players and prerecorded songs that express sadness
    Markers
    Pencils
    Paper
    Candles and candle holders
    Optional: newsprint, tempera paint

Introduction to Topic

Everyone struggles. Life inevitably confronts us with painful times. As Christians we are called to be faithful—even in life's most difficult moments. We need to be reminded that God did not promise a comfortable, trouble-free existence, but we also need to be reminded (again and again) of what God does promise: we will not be alone. God is holding us and molding us all the time. Our Lord provides us hope and life now! And God uses us to bring that message of life to others!

Gathering

Prepare your gathering place. Use a leafless tree branch as a "centerpiece." As participants arrive, play the prerecorded songs for background music. Provide blue construction paper and markers for leaf-tags. Have each person rip construction paper to form a tear-shaped leaf. Then have individuals write their first names on their leaves and how (or why) they are like the bare branches. Provide yarn or string for making loops for attaching the leaves to the branch later.

Form a group circle with the tree branch in the center. Sing Advent hymns, such as "Oh, Come, Oh, Come, Emmanuel," "On Jordon's Bank the Baptist's Cry," or "Comfort, Comfort These My People." Ask God to bless your time together.

As each person shares his or her name and the reason it resembles the bare branch, he or she should place the leaf under the tree. After everyone has responded, use the bare branches as the evening's "object lesson." Read the following paragraphs or put them into your own words.

Discovering

Nature presents many possibilities for parables. By looking, we often see ourselves mirrored in nature.

One such parable is portrayed in bare branches. As the coolness of autumn turns to winter cold, the leaves fall. As the wind tugs, the tightest of leaf-holds eventually gives way to the force of the gusty blast.

All that remains are bleak, bare branches—alone now to weather the winter. A hopeless, dismal, dreary scene?

While summer leaves provide a full, green covering, they hide the inner parts of the tree. Bit by bit, the leaves fall and expose a beauty unseen before. Now, those leafless limbs reveal the intimate, detailed structure of the tree. Take a look; something is attractive about those intimate branches.

Are we mirrored in the trees? Do we prefer people to see us in our "greenery"—the times when we appear courageous, self-assured, and all together? Is it possible that underneath the greatest courage and "all togetherness" are parts of us that struggle and are afraid?

Freedom comes in allowing someone to see our "bare branches." When we share what's really underneath and inside, we begin building extraordinary bonds with others. We honor those friends by revealing our intricacies and intimacies.

It should come as no surprise that our God moves in miraculous and meaningful ways. For "Happy are those who mourn; God will comfort them" (Matt. 5:4). As we share our closely guarded hurts and struggles, we open ourselves to receive care—to experience God touching our lives—through friends. We actually rob someone of the privilege of ministry when we hide our pain!

The Good News doesn't stop there! Leafless does not mean lifeless. In bare branches breathes the promise of spring—the hope of new life. The seasonal cycle teaches us that. The ultimate sacrifice of Christ teaches us that. Isn't it remarkable that we Christians even use the "bare branches" of a cross to remind us of resurrection, joy, and new life! So we live our moments looking beyond and through—discovering light in our darkness, spring in our winters, and Easter in our Good Fridays.

Risking

Crying reflects our greatest joys or deepest hurts. Tears spill when we celebrate the alleluias and struggles through the aches. They become expressions of what's on the inside. Tears are vehicles for viewing someone "inside-out."

One way of sharing "bare branches" is to talk about times of tears. Shuffle the leaves beneath the tree and form small groups by drawing five leaves at a time.

Direct each group of five to build a make-believe bonfire. Use candles, candleholders, and lots of imagination! Dim the lights and gather the groups around their glowing "bonfires." Allow sufficient time for sharing and responding.

Preface the discussion by reminding participants to listen carefully and respectfully. This is an adventure in risk taking. Encourage each person to share only what he or she feels comfortable in revealing! Remember: In expressing our "bare branches," we give others the special privilege of ministering to us.

Begin with the person whose birthday is closest to the first Sunday in Advent. Continue left around the circle as each person uncovers his or her concerns. Use these guidelines for starters and don't be afraid to look underneath and beyond.

    Talking about crying makes me feel . . .
    When a woman cries, I assume/expect . . .
    When a man cries, I assume/expect . . .
    The last time I cried . . .
    The last time I wanted to cry . . .

Occasions that trigger tears . . .
A moving time for me when someone else cried . . .
One person I feel free to cry in front of . . .
I cry alone/with others because . . .
The greatest difficulty I've had to face in my life . . .
The greatest joy I've had to face in my life . . .

Read John 11:28–36 (especially v. 35). What does this verse say about Jesus? about tears? about others? What does this verse say about you?

Supporting

Bring everyone together and decorate the bare branch by hanging the leaves like ornaments. Stand in a circle and divide the group in half. (Do this by going around the circle and "counting off" by saying "sad, glad, sad, glad" in place of numbers.)

Make certain each person has a Bible. Open to the Psalms, a collection and reflection of our human cries. These verses express the emotions of people—helpless and hopeless and filled with praise and promises.

Direct all "sad" team members to search individually for a psalm verse that reflects hurt, need, or pain. "Glad" team members should each hunt for verses of celebration and victory.

For a responsive Scripture reading, form two facing lines with a "sad" opposite a "glad." Begin at one end of the lines, alternating sad and glad verses. Know that in our cries of despair there still resounds the joy of victory.

Now distribute a sheet of paper and pencil to each person. Fold the paper in half. On the top of the page each person should write a one-sentence "psalm of sad." It can be a prayer, need, or concern that reflects a current personal struggle. Place folded sheets under the branch and exchange papers. Now each person should write a response to the prayer need with a word of encouragement, hope, and support.

Join in a close circle, gathered round the branches now laden with leaves and life. As a closing prayer read each person's "psalm of sad" and the Good News response.

Conclude by singing "Hark the Glad Sound! The Savior Comes." Have a hug happening! Make sure everyone gets a chance to give a hug to each person in the room. Reach out as a reminder that we are the ones God uses to touch the lives of those around us. We are the people who share the warmth and encouragement of our Lord's love in times of tears or cheers.

As a reminder, display your tree branch and leaves in the youth room or narthex during Advent.

Celebrating

After praying together, play together. Celebrate the gift of one another by dancing to the prerecorded music that was played at the beginning of the evening.

Or why not give your fingers a chance to dance? Play the taped music and finger-paint expressions of the sounds. Use newsprint to create a giant Advent mural which reflects "comfort in the wilderness" or other Advent season messages.

"Tree-t" Time

For fun, serve assorted fruit that grows on trees—apples, pears, oranges, plums, or other tasty treats. Or go out on a limb: Would pixie sticks be a surprise?

Index

Acceptance

    The Shoelace Acceptance—Do It Now, 74

Advent

    An Advent Ad, 17
    A Time for Giving, 56
    Footsteps and Footprints, 82
    Talking in the Light, 41

Advertising Your Faith

    An Advent Ad, 17

Body

    My Body—My Buddy, 35

Car

    Behind the Wheel, 24

Caring

    Barefootin' and Carefootin', 71
    Shoes . . . I Know Where You're Coming From, 77
    Careful Saints!, 80
    Remember the Able/Disabled, 103
    Ear Wax and Cotton, 106

Choices, Making

    Footsteps and Footprints, 82

Christmas

    Christmas Prayer, 59

Closed Minds

    Closed Minds: Checking Out Prejudices, 14

Communication

    Shoes . . . I Know Where You're Coming From, 77
    Ear Wax and Cotton, 106

Crisis

    Growing Through Grieving, 45
    Life Is Forgiving, 48

Decisions

    Behind the Wheel, 24
    Decisions Involving Jobs, 28

Disabled

    Remember the Able/Disabled, 103

Epiphany

    Day by Day: O Dear Lord, Three Things I Pray, 61
    In Whose Image?, 43

Family

    Family "Is Shoes", 69
    Barefootin' and Carefootin', 71
    The Shoelace Acceptance—Do It Now, 74

Family Trouble

    Family Trouble: The Youth Group as a Friend, 12

Feelings

    The Feelings of Others, 51

Forgiveness

    Life Is Forgiving, 48

Friendship

    Let's Be Friends, 31
    Shoes . . . I Know Where You're Coming From, 77
    Careful Saints!, 80

Giving

    A Time for Giving, 56

Gospel

    Joy: That's Good News, 16

Grace

    Lusty Lady, Cradled Lamb, 45
    Guilty, 100

Grief

    Growing Through Grieving, 45
    Good Grief?, 87

Guilt

    Guilty, 100

Highs and Lows in Life

    Mountains and Valleys, 20

Identity
    It's Not Easy Being Green, 66

Images
    In Whose Image?, 43

Job
    Decisions Involving Jobs, 28
    I Am My Job, 113

Joy
    Joy: That's Good News, 16

Light and Darkness
    Stumbling Around in the Dark, 39

Listening
    Ear Wax and Cotton, 106

Loneliness
    Loneliness: Is Anybody Listening? Does Anybody Care?, 11

Money
    Money Is Power?, 110
    Give It All You've Got, 54

Outrage
    Outrage: Lord, What Can We Do to Help?, 13

Prayer
    Christmas Prayer, 59

Prejudice
    Closed Minds: Checking Out Prejudices, 14

Relationships
    Good Grief?, 87
    Called to Comfort, 90
    See also Friendship.

Relationships, Broken
    Life Is Forgiving, 48

School
    Stress and School, 85

Sexuality
    My Body—My Buddy, 35

Sexuality and Dating
    Let's Be Friends, 31

Sharing
    A Time for Giving, 56

Social Concerns
    Outrage: Lord, What Can We Do to Help?, 13

Stewardship
    Give It All You've Got, 54

Stress
    Success with a Capital "S", 93
    My Success Goal, 96

Transfiguration
    Mountains and Valleys, 20

Troubles
    Bare Branches—A Chance to Cry, 116

Witnessing
    Talking in the Light, 41
    An Advent Ad, 17
    Lusty Lady, Cradled Lamb, 97